EBURY PRESS

UNLOVED

Harshita Gupta is a dynamic and multitalented artist who began her journey as a radio personality and has since become a prominent comedy content producer across all major social media platforms.

In 2023, Harshita's remarkable influence in the digital world earned her a coveted spot on *Forbes India*'s List of Top 100 Digital Stars. Her stories on platforms like Tape A Tale have touched the hearts of millions, showcasing her exceptional storytelling prowess. This is her first book.

Harshita Gupta

Unloved

The Art of Moving On

HARSHITA GUPTA

EBURY
PRESS

An imprint of Penguin Random House

EBURY PRESS

Ebury Press is an imprint of the Penguin Random House group of companies
whose addresses can be found at global.penguinrandomhouse.com

Published by Penguin Random House India Pvt. Ltd
4th Floor, Capital Tower 1, MG Road,
Gurugram 122 002, Haryana, India

First published in Ebury Press by Penguin Random House India 2024

10 9 8 7 6 5 4 3 2

ISBN 9780143468486

Typeset in Sabon by MAP Systems, Bengaluru, India
Printed at Thomson Press India Ltd, New Delhi

www.penguin.co.in

Contents

Preface

I find it rather ironic that I am writing this on Valentine's Day, 2024. In the past ten years, my life has gone through unimaginable changes. My hopes and dreams shifted. As I came alive and became comfortable in my skin, I grew to understand who I am and what I like. I found out that my ideas of love, relationships and romance—primarily moulded by movies and books—are at odds with the real world. And that brings me to why I wanted to write this book—to make sure people don't give up on love. As someone who has navigated the twists and turns of love's labyrinth, I've witnessed first-hand why people often surrender to its complexities. The sting of repeated heartbreaks, the fear of exposing one's vulnerabilities, external pressures dictating our worth, self-doubt whispering in our ear and the exhausting drill of modern dating culture can all erode our belief in love's promise. These personal battles can leave us feeling weary and disillusioned, leading us to question if the quest for love is worth the effort. Why make the effort of asking about someone else's day when you have had a bad one? It might all end in nothingness, or worse, you might be ghosted. In the times we live in, disillusionment is the new norm. Look around you—everyone has a heartbreak tale to tell. Hiding their pain behind a smile and knowing what it feels like to be shattered, they say, 'Never again will I put myself in a place where someone can cause me so much pain.' And somehow, a few weeks, months or years later, they all try again.

It has taken me three decades of being on planet Earth to come to terms with the fact that we are all a little broken inside. It is human to want to give up and equally human to not.

Unloved is my attempt at decoding love. I want to make you all feel a little less lonely by reminding you that we have all been there. When love slips through our fingers, it leaves behind a mountain of emotions that weigh heavy on the heart. Post-break-up pain becomes a cruel reminder of our perceived inadequacies. We question our worth and replay every misstep and flaw with agonizing clarity. Rejection ignites a fiery mix of anger and resentment, directed both inward and outward, as we struggle to make sense of why we need to end up alone, yet again. As we grapple with the harsh reality of being unchosen and unloved, the lingering feeling is one of loneliness. Yet, as human beings, we are designed for resilience—a glimmer of strength that whispers, 'This too shall pass.'

This book couldn't have happened with just my *vishesh tippani*[1] so I brought on board the one person who got me through it all—Anindita Chatterjee, a mental health practitioner, who I am fortunate enough to call a friend today. AC, as I fondly call her, is a long-term confidante (and not my therapist, so no ethical violation here), who helped me make sense of who I am. One of the most important lessons she taught me and I want you all to remember is that the first step to love begins with the exploration and awareness of one's 'self'.

So, as we move through the pages of this book and go through the deep, dark alleys of our hearts, revisit our pain and smile a bit at the happy memories, just remember to never stop loving love and yourself. I promise you, it gets better!

Love,
HG

---

[1] Special comments.

Prologue

2021

It's 8 a.m., Monday.
I am a pile of tears on the floor.
The numbness that began in my shaking hands
has made its way through my veins, stiffening my
muscles to stillness. I break a sweat in the chill of
January. My heart beats out of my chest so fast that
I wonder if it is beating at all.

A plea weighs on my lips, sealing them shut with
the knowledge that no help will come. With
trembling fingers, I tap at my phone. The phone
numbers of distant acquaintances seem blurry on the
illuminated screen.

I need to talk to someone.
I need someone to talk to me.

I want to scream but find no voice. It is as if those early hours of the morning stand hovering over me like an invigilator in the examination hall. If I make a sound, some part of me knows I will fail.

Fifty-eight seconds to go before I am on air.
Fifty-eight seconds to find something to say.

The news headlines scream at me from the open window on my laptop.

There was an accident on the highway. Expect delays.
Forty seconds to go.

Oil prices hit a two-month high. Ride your bike to work.
Thirty seconds to go.

The sky is overcast. 90 per cent chance of rain showers.

Twenty seconds.
My breath comes in wild heaves.

Ten seconds.
Strong winds coming in from the southeast.
The words blur and melt away, taking what little meaning they had with them.
5 . . .

4 . . .
3 . . .
The blinking red light turns green and my hand goes for the LIVE button out of reflex.

The radio voice takes over.
Gooooood morning, Lucknow!

Mausam ka haal behaal hai, barish ka asaarr hai, gharon se chatri ke bina na nikle—because remember, office *mein rainy day nahi hota janemann!* (The weather is in a bad state, it's raining, so don't leave your homes without an umbrella—because remember, there's no such thing as a rainy day in the office, darling!)

But radio *mein hota hai!* Coming up—*ekdum bheegta aur bhigota hua gana* (And on the radio, coming up next—a completely drenching song)—'Barso re Megha Megha' by Shreya Ghoshal only on 98.3 Mirchi, It's Hot!

My hand slips, lifeless from the LIVE button. My voice has left me. I am alone again, but not for long.

The tears come back, a cruel companion in my time of despair.

11 a.m.

I wish my city a pleasant day and sound like I mean it, before throwing my things into my bag and escaping to my car. On the ride back home, I drive as if in a dream—or a nightmare that doesn't seem to end.

Chester Bennington belts the words to 'In the End' from my car speakers—words my mind only half hears but believes.

I park my car and float up the stairs in a daze, crawling into bed fully dressed. I lay motionless but wide awake. The tears never seem to stop their relentless barrage.

My pillow is only half-dry when my mother knocks on the door. I am startled awake from my restless sleep, shooting upright like an animated corpse fresh from the coffin. She looks into my dead eyes with the compassion only a mother can show.

From her gaze, I can tell she knows that my world has fallen apart.

She says, 'Everything happens for a reason—the Lord is saving you from more pain.'

Explain that to my broken heart.

I cannot sleep for hours after she is gone. I haven't slept in months.

The white noise and guided meditations do little to help. Sleep has been replaced by a kind of paralysis, each breath bringing me closer to suffocation, each attempt at survival a step closer to death.

My thoughts whirl around my head in a confused hum that never ceases—*How did I end up this way?*

My heart had made my brain weak. I was a coward in the face of the truth. It would take more than courage to accept what had happened to me—to accept what I had done.

My family, concerned, tried every trick in the book. But the old tricks suddenly seemed alien to this weary dog. I could taste their helplessness in the now muted flavours of my favourite ice creams, the countless dinners at my once most beloved restaurants and the hopeful lilt of their voices as we flipped through old photo albums and relived the good old days.

Nothing worked.

My sunshine, the 'Surya' bulb that they once said glowed behind my eyelids, had short-circuited. Only a blackened mess remained.

One day, my phone rang. It was my boss, her voice betraying the mixture of concern and frustration I seemed to detect in the voices of most people I loved these days.

She asked whether I planned on coming to work the following week and whether work was something I thought I could handle. Her voice told me she knew my answer already. Every day brought a new failure.

I told her I didn't feel like myself.

She told me to take some time but reminded me that there was only so much time she could give. It had been five months, and while she would spend every second she could to give me the time I needed, the company didn't have another minute to spare.

Har boss *ka* boss *hota hai.* (Every boss has a boss.)

I resigned two days later.

My work was the only love I had left, but *bewafaai*[2] was never my style.

Life as a performer can be rough. When the lights go on, so do you. That's just the life of an artist—you're only as good as your worst day, and the audience will never forgive you for it.

Life had begun to feel like the second act of a Bollywood movie. The tragedy had struck, and with all the love songs sung, the script had taken on a more melancholic tone.

---

[2] Betrayal.

Chalte chalte yunhi ruk jata hun main,
Baithe baithe yahi kho jata hun main

(While walking, I stop just like that,
While sitting, I get lost right here)[3]

I had been paralysed, rendered motionless in anticipation of the happy ending. My feelings banged against the door of my waking mind, pounding my skull in the form of a headache.

Cowering in the darkest corners of my consciousness, I would pretend I didn't hear it. I promised myself I would never answer that door.

Instead, I escaped, bounding through the open window of my browser, into the world of sitcoms and movies. My playlist, once singing of wanting 'Something Just Like This', now played the wilting melodies of 'Cigarettes after Sex'.

Jab We Met, my go-to comfort film, now took on a darker tone. I found myself an unwitting Geet in the dramatic saga of my own life, but even Kareena must not have cried as much as I did as the words to 'Aaoge Jab Tum' played over my headphones.

One day, as I sat in my fog of gloom, my brother's voice rang in my ears.

It was the same old story. He had wanted a dog for years and would argue his case with much whining

---

[3] From the film *Mohabbatein* (2000).

every few months before his hopes were shot down by our parents.

But I heard him that day. I heard an inkling of that hopelessness and unfulfilled desire in his voice that reminded me of my own. For the past six months, my brain, tired from the constant banging on the door, had taken a back seat. My heart did the thinking.

Two hours later, I sat beside my brother, a triumphant smile on his face and a month-old Golden Retriever puppy in his lap, as we drove home from the adoption centre. A brand-new doghouse rattled in the back seat, packed with a few empty bowls, a fresh bag of dog food, squeaky toys and a blanket we bought to keep Coco, as we named him, warm through the cold winter months.

My parents were furious. My paternal grandmother (*Dadi*) was terrified of dogs, my dad hated the smell and my mother was livid at the thought of picking stray strands of fur off the kitchenware.

But something inside me had shifted.

The hollowness that had plagued my home suddenly felt fuller, with Coco wagging his tail at the centre of it all.

I remember his first night at home as if it were only yesterday. I held him so tight as I cried into his soft fur that I was half-afraid I would crush him. I prayed a silent prayer that this would be it—this little pup would be my saviour and the only love and salvation that I would need to make the pain go away.

Over his first month at home, Coco became my companion. We would wake up together, eat together, watch TV together, and at the end of the day, curl up beside each other and fall asleep, exhausted. Over time, Coco began to heal me, reminding me that the default state of a soul is to be happy and content with what it has.

But deep down, I knew something was still missing.

I knew I would never be truly happy again until I healed, until the banging inside my skull ceased, and silence took its rightful place.

I had to accept reality, but I wasn't ready.

February 2021

For my birthday, I bought myself tickets to Goa with a friend. In my own small way, this was my *ja, jee le apni zindagi* (go live your life) moment.

My friend, no stranger to the gloom that had taken over my life, decided that with enough alcohol and partying, she could heal me. She wasn't entirely wrong.

For the next few days, we drank and danced the nights away, swiping through eligible bachelors on

Hinge, like the stereotypical rebound phase that follows the dramatic break-up in every chick flick.

Every night, the pain would come. Every night, I would drink until I was numb to it.

I would drink, and drink some more, and brave the waves of uncertainty and pain like a resolute boulder on stormy seas.

But every crashing wave was a reminder of the love in my heart that once had opened a world of possibility.

One drunken night, I decided to revisit the pain I had shut myself to.

The words came like a deluge, and with no one to speak to, I followed my therapist's advice and put pen to paper, writing the words I wished I could say but knew were better left unsaid.

That night, I wrote the last words I ever wanted to say to him. I left a part of myself in those pages, a part of my heart I decided I would never need again.

Dear Diary,

It's over!

Seven years—*seven long years* of togetherness— and the most beautiful chapter of my life has come to an end.

The most beautiful friendship I ever had has been compromised, and it was my fault.

Everyone around me told me he was a fucked-up person, a losing game. They all told me I was making the wrong choice, but choice *toh* choice *hoti hai na?* (Choice is choice, after all, right?)

Meri tum the—galat hi sahi (You were my choice—even if wrong).

I always thought we'd work it out, and believe me, I tried my hardest. I gave it my 200 per cent, even when I had nothing to spare. I gave every inch of my heart, every sliver of love it had left, but alas, some things just aren't meant to be, I guess.

But you never treated me right.

You should have treated me better. After all, I am was your best friend. That's the only *shikayat*[4] I have.

Pata hai (You know)? When I kissed you for the first time and started crying, I could never explain why. But the truth is, I had mixed emotions. I had never felt so safe, so satisfied, so happy—as if it was the beginning of something new.

Who would have imagined it was the beginning of the end?

I remember the way you jumped around and danced that day on your terrace when I hit

---

[4] Grouse.

50k followers on Instagram. You kissed me and said I deserved so much more than this, and that you were sure I would achieve it all. I had never seen someone so happy on my behalf—someone celebrating my success as if it were their own because, in a way, I guess it was.

In so many ways, it was your faith in me that kept me going and fighting for more, for better. It was you that kept me from giving up. I will never be able to thank you enough for that.

You were always more than a friend to me. You were my confidant, my happy place, my partner in crime and my go-to person for everything.

Shayad ab main kabhi Munna *ke yahan gol gappe khane nahi jaaungi, na hi* Shubham *ke yahan* cigarette *lene* (Maybe now I will never go to Munna's place to eat gol gappas, nor to Shubham's place to buy cigarettes)—not because I'm quitting (even you couldn't break me that badly) but because I can't bear to hear him say, '*Arey, aaj bhaiya nahi aaye?*' (He didn't come along?)

For four years, I spent every day by your side. I wonder what I will fill my days with now.

Pata nahi ab office *ke baad kahan jaaungi.*
Pata nahi ab sutta break *kiske sath lungi.*
Pata nahi ab thand ke mausam mein chai Maggi *kiske sath* share *karungi,* meme *kise bhejungi,*

moon emoji *spam bhej ke* irritate *kisko karungi,*
apne video ideas *kis se* discuss *karungi?*
Marvel movies *kaun samjhayega mujhe?*
Mere ladko ki choices *pe kaun judge*
karega mujhe?
Meri cigarette *kaun jalayega? Woh toh hum*
dono ek dusre ki jalate the, na?
Pata nahi yaar . . . Is shehar mein rahi toh move
on *kaise kar paungi?*

(I don't know where I'll go after office now.
I don't know with whom I'll take *sutta*[5] breaks
now. I don't know with whom I'll share chai
and Maggi in the cold weather, to whom I'll
send memes, who I'll irritate with moon emoji
spam, with whom will I discuss my video ideas?
Who will explain Marvel movies to me? Who
will judge me for my choices in guys? Who will
light my cigarette? We used to light each other's,
right? I don't know, man . . . If I stay in this city,
how will I be able to move on?)
That's why I'm leaving the city.

Sabse dur.
Har memory *se dur.*
Har apne adde se dur.
Tum se dur.

---

[5] Cigarette.

(Far away.
Away from every memory.
Away from every hangout spot of ours.
Away from you.)

I won't contact you again. There won't be any more problems because of me. I never thought I would run out of words to write to you, but today, my vocabulary runs dry.

This is it!

This is where our paths diverge, and now, I won't have you as a co-passenger by my side for the road ahead.

I don't know if I will ever love the same way again, but that's not your fault.

I will miss you and love you, hoping with all my heart to stop one day.

From now on, I will light my own cigarettes.

Love,

Junior *Patti*.[6]

2023

It's 8 a.m., Monday.

Two years have passed. The birds are chirping outside. The sun shines through my kitchen window as I make my eggs, sunny side up. Taylor Swift

---

[6] Card.

plays on the radio, and I turn the volume up as high as it goes.

The bell rings, and a man hands me flowers. The card is from my not-so-secret admirer.

So much has changed in the last two years.

From crying alone on the studio floor to greeting my followers on Instagram, a million strong, every morning; from debilitating panic attacks that made my heart feel like it would pop to popping champagne bottles for even the slightest occasion; from broken friendships marred by betrayal to celebrating my bachelorette in Vietnam with my ride-or-dies; and from nearly giving up on love to deep-diving into preparations for my own *big fat Indian wedding*, where I will marry the love of my life. In those places between the bad and the good, a new Harshi was born. The girl who lurked in the shadows of past heartache rose like a phoenix drawn to the light. I emerged anew, someone none of my friends or family could recognize.

Someone stronger, better and brighter than even a Surya bulb.

But what changed?
How did I do it?
Where did the old me go?

Let's start at the beginning . . .

1

The Cardinal Mistake of Falling in Love with My Best Friend

Emily Bronte sold a very specific brand of love to us. 'Whatever our souls are made of, his and mine are the same'. It might be too late, but I have to say to the next generation of women—don't listen to her. I tried it, and it didn't go very well.

I met somebody—my other half, you could say. I dated him. And guess what? Love is the most beautiful lie, and pain is the ugly truth.

Oh, wait! I promised you a story at the end of my prologue. Here is that defining tale of my life, the one that revealed what I am made of. We all have several of these stories. Remember when you stood up to your bullies? Remember when you told off your toxic relatives? Remember when you quit that job you really needed because dignity mattered more than money? Mine would be this above all

1

the others—when I lost my best friends and found myself instead.

We are going to call him Aman in this book. He was my best friend's brother at first. It wasn't love at first sight. I have no idea who came up with the theory that love can happen in a snap. I don't think it can. The only dude who can make a snap work is Thanos and we are neither superheroes nor supervillains, just mere mortals.

I had known Aman for a long time; since we were aimless young people with no sense of purpose in life. We were best friends for eight years. I was a permanent fixture at his home. I was the second daughter his parents couldn't stop doting on. Instead of coming back home from work, I would be at his. His sister Rachana (name changed) was like a sister to me. She and I were inseparable.

As is common in small-town India, growing up in the same neighbourhood inevitably meant that our paths were bound to cross. However, Aman and I had coexisted comfortably for the first fifteen years of our lives without being in each other's orbits. It was Rachana who was my person. He just happened to be there. He and I went to different schools, different colleges, belonged to different worlds and had different social circles. We were even dating different people!

There was nothing common—except Rachana, and of course, our common love for sutta. Smoking is indeed injurious to health and so was he.

Sometime in 2011, Aman and I exchanged our first proper friendly sentences. It must have been about cigarettes or a lighter! We had sneaked out of his cousin sister's wedding to give ourselves some breathing space. Indian weddings, lavish and gorgeous, often attract loud, garish and mostly judgemental people. Aman and I found the atmosphere a little hard to stomach. That evening, away from the loud wedding songs at the party, the two of us had the most comforting conversation about our lives. In that split second, it felt like I had found a friend with whom I could be completely myself—no judgement, no hate, no eye rolls. He just simply got me.

It was a difficult time for both of us. Rachana had moved to a different city for higher education and we had no one else to hang with. Aman was left alone to survive in the wilderness of awkward social settings. He lucked out when I came into his social fold. I was that extrovert who adopted the shy, introverted him. We started meeting each other every day—sutta breaks were mandatory for the soul.

Now hold your horses—all of you out there who will be quick to jump in and say, *ek ladka aur ladki kabhi dost nahi ho saktey* (a boy and a girl can never be friends), zip those lips already!

Many of the movies, TV shows and books we grew up on led us to believe that men and women can't be friends. We have perpetuated, fostered and propagated this idea with such conviction that it has only led to further doom and despair. Men and women are capable of being great friends without letting any sort of attraction come between them. Aman and I would have done just that—continued to be great smoke buddies, have chai together every evening and go back to our own respective lives.

But there was a third person in the mix. His then-partner Shroo (very shrewd). Our society can be quite the breeding ground for women's insecurities. '*Arey uski lagam qas ka thaam rakho, kahin fisal na jaye . . .*' (Hey, hold the reins tightly, make sure he doesn't slip . . .) This lagam led to Aman lying to Shroo—day in, day out. And not just about me.

Have to give it to her—she ran a tight ship. Aman wasn't 'allowed' to have any female friends. It was a rule that could neither be negotiated nor circumvented. And because she lived in another city, the easy route for Aman to have normal, healthy friendships with other kindred souls who weren't his girlfriend was by lying.

Now, sisters, don't worry. I am not with the mister on this one. Lying in a relationship is symptomatic of a much larger issue. There's something that's broken and needs fixing. For the many years that Aman and I remained friends, I never endorsed his lying. It is inexcusable, no matter what's causing it. Now and then, I'd tell him to address it. But for Aman, it was easier to escape it. Or escape all conversations about this.

I would show him my other friends and joke, 'Leave that one. She gives you too much grief. I will find you someone better.' Aman found my bindaas attitude very cool. I was chill and everything he was seeking from life at the time.

Toxic relationships can be lonely and isolating. For a long time, I attributed his decision to stay with Shroo to his desire to avoid confrontations. It must be hard for introverts, I reasoned with myself.

Also, I wasn't blind to the fact that long-distance relationships in our early twenties can be difficult. I was in one too. Transparency is the key to making the road less bumpy. My then-boyfriend was in Delhi and he knew everything about my whereabouts. We both put in the needed effort to make it work.

For Shroo, my existence in Aman's life came as a rude shock. She had come over to surprise Aman at his home and I was having my usual evening chai on his couch after work. It had become a daily routine—I'd finish work and head over to his place for my *shaam ki* chai,[1] do some *gupshup*[2] and then

---

[1] Evening tea.
[2] Gossip.

come home. That day, when Shroo 'caught' me there, I found myself entangled in their showdown. In a fit of rage, Shroo said too many uncalled-for things. I had to leave to not hear any more of the darts directed at me. A few innocent Parle-G biscuits and my harmless cup of chai didn't deserve her bad behaviour.

With a lot of retrospection, I can safely say that Shroo's behaviour could have been avoided. Although it was exaggerated, it was not entirely wrong. She had been lied to. We have a warped notion of what cheating entails. In practical terms, emotional cheating is still cheating. It was just as unfair for Aman to lie to her, as it was for him having to live with the diktat of not having any female friends around. I say this with no judgement, but as I state the facts, it's clear—he deserved better, she deserved better and they both deserved better in their lives.

I wish Shroo had found the courage to leave him that day. But she didn't. And at the time, I didn't understand why she just couldn't leave a man who was simply not present for her.

I found my answers eventually. But this story gets romantic before we get to that.

2020 was the worst year of my life. I had quit a stable job to move to Mumbai and things hadn't panned out the way I had hoped for. I lost my mental peace and was looking for a job at a time when the world was on the verge of a global shutdown. I had wanted to become a comedy writer, but it was the universe pulled a fast one on me.

Within six months, I had exhausted my savings. My mother would call me every day. She was worried I'd end up doing something to myself. I would be home alone all day while all my flatmates went to work. Loneliness was eating me up. Around the same time, my boyfriend and I were drifting apart. We had been together for six years, but it took me a while to muster the courage to say the words, 'I have fallen out of love'. Eventually, I gathered the courage and broke up with him. So, I didn't have a job, money or love.

There was a palpable void in my life—long relationships had become a habitual part of it. Seeking companionship was more about the comfort of knowing someone was around. The break-up, coupled with my career stagnation during the peak of the pandemic, was beginning to make me feel like I had hit rock bottom!

I returned to Lucknow during the pandemic. And there was Aman, right there, with the warmth of his banter, holding out a packet of overpriced cigarettes. Friends can make everything better. And now that I was single, I felt differently about Aman.

Perhaps it was the void in my heart, my need to heal quickly, a rebound attraction or what Aman had told me at Pune airport, the last time we had met in 2019. His words were: 'There is something between us that feels unfinished.'

WHAT?

He had girded his emotions carefully, even the night before, sandwiching his words between copious amounts of whisky. 'I want to kiss you,' he had said. I laughed it off. Sometimes, alcohol makes us say things we don't mean, I'd said in my inebriated state.

The next day at the airport, I didn't get a chance to respond to Aman's words. The moment passed, one of us got distracted and the thought remained unattended.

I hadn't even given it much thought until we reunited in Lucknow. Aman never brought it up again, but clearly, I had too much time to think. It started playing on my mind. Aman was really invested in my life. Knowing how tough it had been for me, he was fully present in a way no one had ever been before.

Aman and I were a magical duo—it felt as if God had sketched us with the same pencil. He was my male doppelganger, understanding me in a way no one else could. Our daily ritual was as predictable as a sunrise: I'd rush over to his place after work for our chai-and-sutta time. Some habits from the old days of our friendship stayed, and we were going to make a few new ones in the days to come.

He, the introvert, and I, the extrovert who had adopted him, made an odd yet perfect pair. It should have made no sense, but somehow did. Our love for golgappas was the glue that sealed this friendship. We devoured them daily, and I mean daily in the truest sense. Our street food vendor knew us so well that if we dared to show up separately, he'd ask, 'Where's your other half today?'

When the winter chill descended that year, we switched our golgappas for piping hot momos and tea, but the sutta remained constant. Aman was not just my smoke buddy, but my partner in crime in everything I did. We were like a comedy duo in our own sitcom, and our daily antics always left us in stitches.

He knew what the break-up was doing to me. And it wasn't just the break-up. It was that time in my life when Murphy's law had taken over. Everything that could go wrong, did go wrong. It was a break-up born out of falling out of love, leaving me with a void. I was emotionally indifferent to the break-up, but it had left a void in my life—a void that began to gnaw at me.

What can a friend do except be there for you at such a time? And Aman was there.

He saw me struggling and, without being asked, stood by my side. With his goofy smile, wild banter and bad jokes, he'd come over and make me watch a web series every day, almost forcing me to when I didn't want to get out of bed, because I wanted to sulk in my despair.

He was there, just like he had always been. We'd always been each other's pillars of support. The web series routine was his way of making me engage with something so I wouldn't fall into the abyss of overthinking. He would follow up with questions related to the series, ensuring I didn't dwell on my thoughts all day long.

He even introduced me to the entire Marvel Universe, patiently explaining the moves and strategies of the *Avengers*. If I was having a tough day or feeling mentally off, he would dedicate his entire day to be there for me. Spending so much time with someone naturally deepens your connection with them.

He would take me out for a drive every evening— we would stop at a *theka*, buy wine and drink in the car. I wouldn't drink with anyone else but him. It was all the same, day after day, but my feelings for him were changing.

Why wouldn't they? Everyone, from the *chaat wale bhaiya*[3] at the *nukkad*[4] to our friends and families would routinely parrot to me, 'You guys

---

[3] The savoury-treats vendor.
[4] Corner from my house.

are so perfect for each other, why don't you two get together?' So much of what happens in our lives is the *bhasad* created by these well-meaning folks. For the strictly English-speaking readers, bhasad means mess. Had it not been for their constant insistence that there was scope for more between us, I wouldn't have seen the 'perfection' in him during that ill-fated phase.

To be fair, look at the optics of the situation. He and I are best friends. His sister is like a sister to me. His family loves me a lot. My family loves his family. It sounds dreamy, doesn't it? Now, when something is that dreamy, it is imperative we look closely at it.

I did try to dodge the inevitable, but I was just not strong enough for the barrage of emotions. One day, while drinking in the car, I felt what he had felt in Pune for me. There were violins in the background and an empty bottle of wine in front of me. All I wanted to do was kiss him! I couldn't wrap my head around why this was happening after eight years.

I couldn't understand why it was happening or what to do about it.

It took me some time to make sense of what I was feeling before I texted him. I told him what I had felt because I thought to myself: It's Aman, for God's sake. He will get it. Aman never rubbished my feelings and neither did he say this is a phase! I think even he was gauging what this is for him. Also, there was Shroo. For the next two weeks, I stayed home and avoided him. The next time we met, I felt it again. This time, there wasn't any wine I could blame. How high can chai make you? It kept on growing.

Every Lucknow kid has their specific *addas*—shady corners that only they know of. Aman and I had our own, of course. On an unusually eventful evening, we met at our corner after a long time. I had missed him. It seemed like he'd missed me. We had the wine with us that he had just picked up. And fuck you, rain gods for starting it all!

I somehow knew what was going to happen that day. At 9 p.m., I got up and said, 'Let's leave; it's getting late.' I knew where it was going. But he wanted to chill some more. The vibe in the air was telling me that this wouldn't end well. There were some silences, many unsaid words and a pile-up of simmering emotions waiting to emerge.

At 10 p.m., I again said, 'I want to go home!' He still didn't want to. We sat there for a while longer. No words, marinating in our own silences. I wasn't even that drunk. Neither was he. We just wanted it. And not just because everyone around us said we should be together. There was something pulling us together, making us feel one with each other. There were years of love, obviously, but now suddenly there was attraction. His smile made my heart somersault. There were butterflies in my stomach whenever he was next to me.

I was playing strong. *No, don't Harshita. There is too much at stake. You'll lose the friendship. He is too precious to be lost!*

But then he smiled. His lips curving made my heart flutter. *It's Aman . . . no matter what happens after this, I can never lose him, right? Fuck it!*

I knew he felt the same way too. In a swift motion, he held me in his arms, and I went for it. We kissed!

We had been fighting alone for a long time. So much bad had happened in my life, in the world around us. That kiss was the kindest, most pure and unaffectedly happy emotion I had felt that year. It was magical. I cried at that moment.

We had both wanted it to happen and had restrained ourselves for a long time. That night, in that kiss, and that quiet drive back home, we allowed ourselves some time away from the carefully constructed 'coulda-shouldas' and be us. It was magical. My heart was full of glee.

The next morning, I woke up feeling really awkward. *It will all be better. Aman and I will make our friendship work. We will . . . we will . . . we will, right?*

I was single. He wasn't. And he couldn't have simply abandoned Shroo one day out of the blue. I respected him for that. He was a good guy, after all.

Aman and I had a long chat about our messy situation and came up with the solution that a casual arrangement is what this will be. But we were foolish enough to not realize that casual relationships exist only between people who don't know each other. When it is two people who have years of friendship behind them, there is too much emotion in the mix for it to be no-strings-attached. This wasn't a wham-bam-thank you-ma'am one-night stand for either of us. We were each other's safe place—*sukoon ghar*.

When the world came crashing down on either of us, we ran into the other's arms. Now with the 'casual' relationship we were attempting, we should have known that eventually hearts would be broken.

Within four weeks, I had feelings for him. Unknowingly, knowingly, willingly, unwillingly, there was no escaping the fact that I was the 'other woman'. I gave an ultimatum—he had to make a choice between Shroo and me.

Aman kept saying he couldn't live without me. So it was clear he would take a hard stand on this and follow his feelings. He devised a plan to ease out Shroo. Now that's the sort of guy he was; he didn't want any wounds.

In the weeks that we had been together, I had become so vulnerable and felt so dependent on Aman that I didn't know how to let him go. So, I followed him on the warped path for the larger good—of finding my happily-ever-after. Aman called Shroo and told her it was not working out and seemingly ended it with her.

And then, our relationship began. It was the beginning of the end.

I don't recall how the preposterous idea of falling for Aman first occurred to me. It had been happening for years, now that I try to remember. Clues were left in lines such as: 'No one knows you better than me.' Factually correct. 'Your family loves me so much.' Again, correct. I have come to the conclusion that our friendship had led me to believe that he was my ultimate happy space. Look, how perfect—two best friends, made of the same soul, will date, marry and live together forever.

I was on cloud nine. Aman and I were inseparable during that phase. We used to brainstorm together for my videos, jam, laugh, and even place bets on which video would go viral. For an entire year, I was stuck at 35k subscribers, and he was the only person on this planet who patiently listened to my frustrations every single day. Not once did he tell me to quiet down or say, 'not today' or 'stop cribbing'. He just quietly listened, offering comfort and sometimes even treating me to delicious golgappas before heading home.

Then, in November 2020, my first video went viral, and my subscriber count reached 49k. I was overjoyed, so much so that I hesitated to open my Instagram app, afraid that I might have already hit 50k. But he encouraged me to check, and when I did, it read 50k. He rushed to the terrace, dancing with exuberance. I could hear the happiness in his voice as he kissed me and said, 'You deserve so much more than this, my love. You've worked incredibly hard.' That evening remains unforgettable. We ordered our favourite food and celebrated in our own understated way, just as we both preferred it. I look back at that day and acknowledge that my success isn't all mine. Aman was there all along making it happen, being a pillar of strength to me. Behind every successful woman, there's a loving partner who not only believes in her dreams but also cheers for her like no one ever can. In Aman, I found that cheerleader, that support system, that caregiver, that partner, that soulmate. He was that missing piece of my heart I had been looking for all along.

I have never been the very fuss and feathers kind of girl. I like simple things, sweet nothings. Effort is attractive to me! In small gestures, you can gauge the attentiveness of your partner. Aman would pick up on all the details. On the first day of 2021, there was a *sundarkaand paath*[5] at my home. As *prashad*,[6] we had bought a few kilos of boondi, my favourite sweet. But I wasn't allowed to eat it because it was a part of *bhog*.[7]

I had spent a whole day cribbing to Aman about how badly I was craving boondi. So he got me the best gift ever—he went all the way to Hanuman Setu, where you get my favourite boondi in the city, and got a whole packet. He met me at our usual evening spot to hang out and handed me a whole *dabba*[8] of boondi. My joy knew no bounds as I ate like a happy schoolgirl who had landed her favourite candy!

Now, for Aman, this was a big gesture. He wasn't someone who moved an inch for anyone, and for a whim of mine, the boy had gone to the other end of the city.

In Aman's world, my every whim was a command, and he'd move heaven and earth to bring my desires to life. Harshita whispered a wish and Aman sprang into action, turning dreams into reality with every beat of his heart. He was my patti and I was his junior patti and that was the bubble we lived in. I am taking the genesis of these names to my grave—there are some secrets that aren't to be spilled. But let's just

---

[5] Recitation of sections of Ramayan.
[6] Offering.
[7] Food for the deity.
[8] Box.

say that we were both fans of *teen patti*.[9] That's the safest answer to give.

In the early days of our relationship, we had crafted a tiny universe all our own, impervious to the harsh realities of the outside world. It was a world where two hearts intoxicated with love could simply cruise through life, carefree and jubilant. Those initial stages of any relationship are truly magical. We were inseparable, two souls so deeply entwined that the world around us faded into the background.

We would embark on aimless drives, the open road serving as the canvas for our adventures. Every moment was a thrill, a shared secret between us. We'd laugh uncontrollably at the silliest things, and time seemed to stretch out, giving us the luxury of being fully immersed in one another's presence.

In those moments, the rest of the world ceased to exist. It was just us, cocooned in our own little universe of love. The outside noise, the concerns of the day, the judgemental gazes of others—all of it faded away. We were lost in the enchantment of our connection, intoxicated by the mere presence of one another.

The longing for each other was insatiable, and there was an almost magical ability to overlook the imperfections. We would spend all day together

---

[9] It is a poker-like card game.

and then the minute we got home, we would be back on call.

It was a time when all that mattered was Aman, and the possibilities of what our love could become.

Now that two such close friends were dating—like a sitcom moment from *Friends,* did they know that we know that they know?

Aman had told me to hold off on telling people. 'We will tell when the time is right. Let's tread with care,' he had said. I mean, of course. Because dating the easiest suspect comes with a whole ton of soap opera, Korean-style drama. All I wanted was some serenity. People fall in love for peace and calm, and here we were sitting around heightened drama.

Shroo told Aman that she would never marry another person if he didn't return. Aman tried to not worry me. He dealt with it alone, holding off Shroo's many thousand calls and the routine breakdown before him.

I wouldn't have known, but she just appeared at my doorstep. Just twelve hours after a perfect day with Aman—we'd watched a movie, snuggled and napped—I was faced with drama.

She broke down in front of me and begged me to let her man go. It might seem to you like a scene from a soap opera. The natural reaction would have been anger, but I stood there feeling very sorry for her. Imagine what we do to our girls that they need to resort to such extreme things to win a man's love. Shroo is a lawyer, a chartered accountancy topper and one of the prettiest girls I have seen in my life. And here she was, wailing to me: 'Please leave him for me. He says he can't live without you, but he is actually mine.' I was in half a mind to give her some of my tough love—do you hear yourself, woman?

This gorgeous woman, who had just been dumped, wanted to be with a guy who couldn't live without me. As you make sense of this tongue twister, I will tell you the most pathetic thing she did. She held out her shawl and begged: 'Just go away from his life.' Seeing her cry bewildered me.

I could never do this for Aman, no matter how deep my love was. I say this with no judgement but genuine concern. How can a woman make herself believe that a guy is the fulcrum of her universe?

I got a sense from Shroo that she'd never let Aman go. If he slept with someone else, she'd say, 'It's okay, it's a mistake anyone can make.' So, when he left her for me, Shroo saw it as a hiccup on her road to happiness. She had full faith in the fact that she would bring Aman back.

I found her misplaced confidence laughable; little did I know the joke was on me.

A few weeks later, I started to sense that something was amiss, and it wasn't just a hunch. I went to Aman's dad's sixtieth birthday party. His friends were teasing me about how I was now a part of the family. My heart was so full that evening. We were all so happy—eating, cheering, dancing, drinking. I wanted to seize the day and that moment. The cops even came in to shut the music at 2 a.m.

At 3 a.m., I heard his phone ringing. Who would call my boyfriend at that ungodly hour? It was Shroo. I was probably drunk, felt betrayed, and I broke down. I wanted to go home at that very moment, but it was late. He somehow persuaded me to stay. But my heart was breaking into a million pieces. What was going on? I went to the bedroom and cried until I fell asleep. It was the first of many such nights in the months to come.

The next day, I had a chat with him. Why was he still talking to her? He said he wasn't and that she just kept calling.

I'm all for being supportive of ex-partners, but daily contact? That's a recipe for never moving on. How they mend their broken hearts is their responsibility. It might sound blunt, but sometimes a clean break is the most compassionate choice for everyone involved.

That incident was the start of my suspicions. Whenever I confronted him with them, he'd dismiss my concerns with a casual, 'Stop overthinking it,

babe. It's not what you think.' He brought up
my once easy-going demeanour as if my growing
unease was a personal failing. 'What happened to
you? You used to be so chill,' he'd say. I couldn't
help but remember how, in the early days of our
friendship, I'd eagerly shared pictures of my friends
and even offered to set him up with them. Why was
my trust slowly eroding?

The contrast between those early days and the
present situation only heightened the sense that
something was seriously amiss.

Aman had become a master at concealing his
actions. He skilfully sidestepped my persistent
questions. A profound anxiety began to take root
within me, making daily life feel like a relentless
struggle. Why was I overreacting? Why was I feeling
this deep desire to snoop on him? Was he hiding
something? And most of all, there was that fear that
I didn't want to confront—the fear that this would
end, and I'd lose him.

A woman's gut feeling is a detective that could
make even Sherlock Holmes jealous. Had he done
anything to make me distrust him? Not really. There
were his ex's calls now and then, but he was honest
about it. He didn't want to drive her over the edge.
He was genuinely worried she'd do something to
herself. They had dated for ten years. How could
I not allow my man to be kind?

Desperate for answers amidst my conflicting
emotions, I sought emotional clarity. I got myself

professional help and began seeing a therapist. I was losing my mind, looking for clues in every action, every word.

But my situation only worsened. I realized that when I got my first crippling panic attack. We were in the car one day and my heart raced as I glanced over and saw his phone illuminated. It was none other than 'Shrooo calling'. The feeling of dread that washed over me in that moment was indescribable, as if the walls of my world were closing in.

My breath quickened, each inhale struggling to reach the depths of my lungs, while the relentless drumbeat of my racing heart echoed in my ears.

An invisible vice gripped my chest, squeezing with an unyielding intensity. Panic welled up like a sinister character, its presence growing with every passing second.

My body trembled as perspiration soaked my trembling palms. It was a single degree in the peak winters of Lucknow, but I was sweating profusely. And my chest hurt like I was having a heart attack. I tried to scream, but my voice was imprisoned by the grip of fear.

It was a terrifying feeling, where panic took centre stage. What was happening?

Aman's presence only seemed to magnify my restlessness. His efforts to comfort me, usually so reassuring, now made me uneasy. I became clingy. I slowly saw myself do things I would never have expected. He was starting to chafe against the raw edges of my nerves. I found myself irritable, my patience worn thin like a frayed thread.

Meanwhile, Shroo's virtual presence meandering around us began to grate on my nerves. Every little sound, every minor disturbance, felt like an assault on my already fragile state of mind. I couldn't help but snap at the tiniest provocations, and my crankiness became an unintended consequence of my anxiety.

In that moment, I longed for solace, but even the most well-meaning gestures and familiar presence didn't help. The soft hum of Aman's voice and the gentle touch of his hand on my shoulder, our car rides and smoke breaks, all of which I had so cherished in the past eight years, were now a backdrop to my growing agitation.

It was as if the world had conspired to amplify my discomfort, leaving me trapped in a swirl of emotions I couldn't easily escape.

I was beginning to take a closer look at what I was into. It was the relationship. Something wasn't right.

I knew it was a conversation I couldn't escape any more. I sat down with Aman and asked him— what did he feel about Shroo and what did he want to do about us? We hadn't told our parents, so now was the time to make a solid decision.

He said, and I still remember it clearly: 'I miss her when I am with you. When I am with her, I miss you.'

I realized what I had known all along in my bones but had done my best to ignore—Shroo was never gone. It struck me like a lightning bolt.

FROM AC'S DESK

'*Darr. Beychaini.*[10] A sudden scary feeling. Almost as if I am falling through an elevator shaft, or the nauseating feeling of being on a roller coaster. Can't explain this, something is happening. My body is reacting, I don't know why I am crying and shaking like this. What's the word, uh, what's the word for it, panic?', that's how a lot of people describe it when they are under the grip of a panic attack for the first time.

We hear the word panic often. At work, at home, on the streets. Where does the word panic come from and is it the same as fear? The word panic was derived from French panique, from modern Latin panicus and from Greek panikos. Greek mythology suggests the word comes from the God Pan, noted for causing terror. He was said to have occasionally caused humans to flee in unreasoning fear, which is where the commonly used sense of panic comes from.

A panic attack is often described as a brief episode of intense anxiety which may cause physical sensations of fear. There are many reported symptoms, namely, racing heartbeat, shortness of breath, dizziness, nausea, tightening of the throat, chills, abdominal pain, sweating, chest pain, trembling and muscle tension. It can

---

[10] Fear and restlessness.

last from a few minutes to even up to half an hour. However, the emotional effects of the attack may last many hours after the episode.

Apart from the physical symptoms, people have often reported experiencing feelings of dissociation as well as a sense of disconnection from reality and the present moment.

Harvard Medical School explains what happens to the body when panic takes hold of our nervous system as follows.[11] When the body is faced with immediate danger, the brain orders the autonomic nervous system to activate the 'flight-or-fight' response. The body is flooded with a range of chemicals, including adrenaline, that trigger physiological changes. For example, heart rate and breathing are accelerated, and blood is shifted to the muscles to prepare for physical combat or running away. A person may experience the symptoms of a panic attack in harmless and apparently stress-free situations, such as watching television or while asleep.

It can be very distressing to experience panic attacks. Breathing deeply from the lungs and exhaling with a sound, ice pack on the back of the neck, sucking ice chips, laying down on

---

[11] Howard E. LeWine, 'Understanding the stress response', *Harvard Health Publishing*, 3 April 2024, https://www.health. harvard.edu/staying-healthy/understanding-the-stress-response.

the stomach and grounding oneself, and getting support from people around can help manage the situation at the time of the incident.

Some reasons for a panic attack can be attributed to chronic stress, change in environment, life transitions, undiagnosed illness and substance abuse, amongst others.

If one has sustained and recurring symptoms of a panic attack, it's very important to see a professional and attend to the underlying reason.

2

The Mess: That's What Rock Bottom Must Feel Like

I remember reading Javed Akhtar's profound words on his marriage with Shabana Azmi. He had said, '*Meri aur* Shabana *ki dosti itni gehri hai ki shaadi bhi hamara kuch nahi bigaad payi.*' (My friendship with Shabana is so deep that even marriage couldn't affect it.)

I firmly believe the bedrock of any happy relationship is a solid friendship. Everything else is built from there. Aman and I were already the best of friends, so one might assume constructing everything else would be a cakewalk.

WRONG.

I am in half a mind to blame friends. For all the balm it is for people who uproot themselves and move to another city—where friends are the family they have—it did me dirty by setting the wrong expectations.

When Aman and I started dating, I had this bloated idea of a fairytale story for us. Because when close friends get together, they end up like Monica and Chandler. They know each other's flaws and they know exactly how to work through them.

I had a checklist and Aman ticked each item on it:

1. Our love was in the comfort of chai and Maggi after a long, hard day at work.
2. He got the difference between my PMS tears, my anxiety tears and my bad-day tears—each very different from the other.
3. It doesn't matter how stupid, ridiculous or innocuous a text was—he would always reply! ALWAYS!
4. I could be 100 per cent me with him.
5. Could be completely silly with each other and take hundreds of funny videos of each other. What's more precious than making prized memories for life . . .
6. Could vent to each other, each day, every day, all day!
7. Could judge the world around us, together. Tripping on this afterwards was a delight.
8. Ate every meal out of the same plate!
9. Completed each other's sentences.
10. Understood each other's silences.
11. Every hug felt like 'where have you been? I have waited a lifetime for you . . .'

12. Were each other's pick-me-up buddy. Problem—anything. Solution—him.
13. And no matter what happened, it was us against the world. We'd always choose each other. Every. Damn. Time!

Now only if number thirteen was as accurate as I'd imagined it to be . . .

We have bloated fantasies of love. All of us do. There are couples we idolize. For some, it could be Rahul and Anjali from *Kuch Kuch Hota Hai*; for others, it might be Bunny and Naina from *Yeh Jawani Hai Deewani*. For me, it was always Monica and Chandler from *Friends*. Aman and my relationship was like the real-life version of it.[12]

Coming back to Aman and me: Yes, we were best friends, always there for each other. But then, one day, our storyline took a dramatic twist, and we both thought, 'Could this be the epic romantic story we've been waiting for?'

Unlike Monica and Chandler, our transition from 'just friends' to 'something more' was less

---

[12] It is sad that as I type out this chapter, I have heard of the untimely demise of our beloved Matthew Perry. Chandler lives in our hearts, but for me, the actor's death was truly the end of an era.

exhilarating and more nerve-wracking. We had found a hidden plot twist in our script that we couldn't resist exploring.

But what sitcoms don't tell you is that at the receiving end of the comedic misunderstandings and plot twists is a person who is crumbling. Chandler's adorable moments of doubt and witty banter aren't charming when you must live with it. It's infuriating. The laughs and inside jokes were drying up for Aman and me. Our vibe was changing. I was persistently tense now and the endearing love that drew us to each other was slowly dissipating in the face of our troubles.

My reality proved to be a tad more complex. While *Friends'* portrayal of friendships evolving into lasting romantic bonds is heart-warming, real-life relationships come with their own problems. The line between friendship and romance can blur and managing the shifts in expectations can become a delicate balancing act. But that wasn't what was wrong. I was a victim of my own expectations. *Friends*, as entertaining as it may be, sold to me that love and companionship among friends is a beautiful thing.

This story turned out to be a lesson in how reality isn't always neatly scripted.

After that conversation with Aman about how he wasn't entirely done with Shroo, my mind started working overtime. Anxiety can make you look for reassurance in places where the reality can't be starker. You desperately want to have hope, and believe in sunshine and unicorns. For me too, it became an exercise in trying to find clues that I would win in the end.

I am an advertising student. I have forever lived in a land where ones and zeros converge . . . there lies an unwavering truth that data is the silent sentinel of reality. It neither distorts nor veils. It bears the weight of evidence and is unburdened by interpretation or sentiment. Data is an impartial witness. Amid the complexities of my relationship, I saw data as an anchor upon which I would decide Aman's and my future during my insomniac spell that night.

So, I drew out a strengths, weaknesses, opportunities and threats (SWOT) analysis report. I was taught that this was a strategic planning tool that helped organizations or individuals assess their strengths and weaknesses and opportunities and threats. So, let's look at the grade sheet of Aman and Harshita:

Strengths:

1. Compatibility
2. Understanding
3. Respect
4. Career support and inputs

Weaknesses:

1. Indecisiveness
2. Courage to take a stand
3. Lazy and always in comfort zone
4. Lack of effort
5. Moody
6. Lack of focus and passion

Opportunities:

1. No need to start searching for new love
2. Financial stability

Threats:

1. Negative influences—pests we know!
2. Shroo
   i   Very uncertain
   ii   Might cause trouble in future
3. Threat to career growth
4. Emotional instability
5. Stuck in the same city that I grew up in
6. Restrictions in social circle

Conclusion

(I read to myself in the most business-like analytical voice at 3.25 a.m. one morning.)

The SWOT analysis of Aman and Harshita reveals several key insights. Their strengths include compatibility, understanding, respect and the presence of career support. However, they also possess notable weaknesses, including his indecisiveness and a lack of focus and passion.

Despite their weaknesses, there are definite potential opportunities for improvement. Aman and Harshita may not need to start from scratch as there is enough ground to build something strong on. On the flip side, they face several threats that could hinder their growth.

Overall, Aman and Harshita's SWOT analysis highlights the need to leverage their strengths, address their weaknesses, capitalize on available opportunities, and devise strategies to mitigate the identified threats to achieve personal and professional success.

You might be muttering to yourself that I was losing my mind, right? Yes, you are right! Overthinking became an unintended workout regimen that left me drained but never took me any closer to the tranquility of the finish line.

The truth, no matter how hard I tried to deny it, was that Shroo was always lurking in the background.

She never left the scene. Aman and she had a complex equation. They barely spoke in the day, maybe for a few minutes, but never quite enough. After he told me that he did miss her sometimes, I started stalking with such vehement passion that I could be hired as a spy. Women are like detectives with an intuition upgrade—they can uncover hidden secrets even if they are stashed somewhere deep below the earth's core.

I started tracking what time Shroo would be online and matched it with Aman's. There were days when I could see them online at the same time for long spells and I would start hyperventilating. I knew they were talking. After a few days, I asked him if he had been talking to her. The good thing about Aman is that he was honest. But what do I do with honesty if I don't like the answer? 'Yes, she has been very low,' he would say. 'I am not comfortable with it, Aman,' I would say. He would immediately soothe my feelings. 'I know. But you must understand, I can't simply abandon her. She and I were together for more than a decade. I have to be there for her.'

Aman's response hit me hard every time. Shroo was always going through something, and he always had to be there for her! I knew he was a kind and caring person, and his loyalty was one of the things I admired. But at the same time, it made my anxiety skyrocket. Does it count as cheating if I knew about it?

I was conflicted; I didn't want to be the one to come between him trying to do the right thing, but I couldn't ignore the unease it was causing me. I could feel the anxiety and the uncertainty within me whenever Shroo's name came up.

'Is it that you don't trust me?' Aman once asked me, a hint of concern in his voice. 'Is that what this is about?' We were in an argument. Or maybe it was a bad day. We were frequently having bad days; they were coming fast at me.

There was no apparent reason to not trust him. He always kept me in the loop. But it was also hard for me to watch Aman talking to his ex-girlfriend frequently. It was not about doubting intentions; it was more about my own middle-class morality that believes in fidelity. I'd wonder, 'How do they move on if they never cut off?'

I've grown up with certain expectations about relationships—monogamy being the primary one. I never had a close relationship with my exes after we broke up, and I guess I was trying to make sense of this different dynamic. I am not saying exes can't be friends. Oh, they can be. But Shroo wasn't a friend to Aman. She was unable to let go of the man she thought was the love of her life.

But I didn't want to be the one who told him who he could or couldn't talk to. Who was I to tell him that? I was not Shroo . . . And then, I saw myself metamorphose further into a person I didn't recognize. Was I becoming Shroo?

The red flags I loathed in her were all beginning to appear in me:

Controlling (Check)
Stalking (Check)
Insecure (Check)
Irritable (Check)

What was wrong with me? I didn't have the courage to verbalize it succinctly then. I have it now—I was living in an illusion. It was always enticing but always just beyond my grasp. From a distance, it seemed like an oasis of love. Yet, as I drew nearer, it revealed itself as a trick of the heart.

We saw glimpses of what we wanted, but the closer we got, the more the truth showed itself. Our connection was just a glimpse of what could have been.

It took me a while to admit it to myself, let alone to him, and now to the world—Aman and Harshita's love story was turning out to be a big, fat lie.

During those trying last days of being in it, my heart could no longer bear the weight of my emotions.

My journal became both my confidant and my
solace. In those three long months, I had shed not
only tears but also a considerable amount of weight.

My days were filled with profound sadness and
I often found myself weeping like a soul who had
lost her way, seeking solace in the presence of a man.
I felt as if my very life depended on his presence,
a desperation that consumed me and overshadowed
my sense of self.

I would fill pages and pages in a day, marking
them with anguished cries for a better time.
Journaling is like having a secret conversation with
yourself, except you're a terrible secret keeper, and
you always spill the beans to yourself. Today, the
journals serve as proof of my lunacy.

*Beinteha pyaar mein pagal ho jana koi mujh se
sikhey . . .*
(Someone should learn from me how to go crazy
in boundless love . . .)

Sample this entry, for instance:

Things not in my control:

1. Aman chooses Shroo
2. People moving away from my life
3. Career growth

Things in my control:

1. Talking to Aman
2. Making travel plans
3. Shopping/Saving
4. Prioritizing family
5. Trusting him

I would write like a kid in primary school, punished by the class teacher.

Here's another one . . .

Repeat after me:

1. I won't overthink
2. I won't overthink
3. I won't overthink
4. I won't overthink
5. I won't overthink
6. I won't overthink
7. I won't overthink
8. I won't overthink
9. I won't overthink

There was a time when I wanted to make it work so badly that I made notes about it in my journal:

1. He needs time
2. I don't want to rush things
3. I don't want to poke him for commitment unnecessarily

4. I want to give him space
5. I want him to be 100 per cent sure about me
6. Wait till therapy begins
7. Giving him time is my decision and I stand by it
8. I have to let it go for a while

I would sometimes sit alone, clutching my old journal, the pages weathered by time. As I flipped through the entries, each turn of the page unveiled a haunting spectre from my past.

I felt a chilling detachment from the person I once was. It was as though Harshita, the one who had penned these words, had faded into oblivion. Who was this person? This couldn't be me.

A bitter smile would tug at the corners of my lips as I read on, realizing how trivial my past actions seemed now. I often pondered how I could have ever allowed myself to engage in such petty endeavours. I questioned the choices I made and the words I had written. I really mocked my older self.

I would never do this for anyone else in life any more. My eyes were once filled with naivety, but now I blazed with passion, rage and mostly faith in myself that I would never let myself compromise my self-respect and self-worth ever again.

That old version of myself was sealed away forever. Harshita had indeed died. But from the ashes of her former self emerged a stronger, wiser and more self-aware person. The pettiest chapter of my past had been closed, never to be revisited.

Every day since then, I found these pages to be a perpetual reminder that even amid my darkest days, I was always better than my worst moments.

A snap between us was inevitable.

It was all brewing inside me until one day, I knew I had reached my breaking point. My life, in three months, had plunged to an unimaginable low. I found myself utterly unable to believe it. Was this truly the life I had been destined for? Who had I become? What was the meaning of this relationship that had grown so twisted and complicated? I questioned every aspect of my existence.

Then came the moment when I knew this was it. He callously revealed to me that Shroo was on his mind and so was I. He couldn't pick one person. He loved us both.

I was no more than an expendable option in his eyes. This man dared to see me as an inconsequential figure. The very fact that there was a choice to make was when I made the resolute decision to excuse myself from the equation. Let's simplify this tormenting complexity of our entangled love lives.

We had a tradition of doing COC—cigarette over call. This was the last time we'd be doing this or anything together. I braced myself for it. Till date, breaking up with him has been the hardest thing I've ever had to do. I didn't have the words.

So, I told him the first thing that came to my mind. Much to my disbelief, the words in my heart were: 'I don't want to be with you.' The most difficult sentence to have ever come out of my mouth, but someone had to have the courage. It was clear Aman didn't have the spine to do so.

That was the last time I heard his voice. However, he did try calling, texting and meeting me. He lived a lane away from my house, so it wasn't easy. I stopped going to our usual haunts. I would avoid our common cigarette guy, the person we bought our snacks from, common friends—anyone who could hinder my moving on.

Within a month of our separation, while he was endlessly texting me, I found out that he and Shroo 'officially' got back together. I couldn't bear the pain of being 'officially' separated from the man I loved so wholeheartedly, but I knew I had to be resolute in my decision. Aman would have continued swinging between me and Shroo, and I didn't want to wait around for a man who couldn't make up his mind.

When I began reflecting on his behaviour, I realized, he was, in many ways, utterly spineless. It was as if he perpetually straddled the middle ground, never fully committing to any stance or decision. Be it in personal relationships or broader matters, he seemed permanently trapped in a state of indecision. He hesitated when support was needed and was unwilling to take a strong stand for anyone, including himself. This lack of conviction in his character created a perpetual sense of frustration and disappointment, leaving those around him yearning for the kind of loyalty that he was incapable of.

The spinelessness left a void in the trust I placed in him.

That night, I wrote in my journal . . .

In matters of love, I choose not to wait,
For a man who's fickle, I'll close that gate . . .

Somehow, when nothing works out, Goa helps. Failed an exam—go to Goa. Had your heart broken—Goa. Ran out on your wedding day—Goa. Basically, no matter what the problem is, I'm convinced the solution lies in Goa. In my case, I just wanted to be in lanes where I wouldn't run the risk of bumping into Aman. I was free, around my girlfriends, hopping from cafe to cafe and endlessly staring at the vast seas, and hoping that my pain would feel like a speck in front of its immense span. I sat at a quiet beach looking at the sky and prayed hard that the pain in my heart would subside a bit.

February 2021

It was my birthday that week, and to ring in my big day, my girls took me out. We went to a modest shack on Calangute beach that served potent drinks and played groovy music. I was staring at my phone, gazing at Aman's number. I wanted to know why he didn't do better; why he didn't put in the effort. Yes, I needed some sort of closure. A grand finish to this grand love story I had spun in my head—where my best friend and I ended up together.

Let me drop some wisdom on you: Closure is the VIP party of life and you're the bouncer holding the list. It's all about letting yourself in. No one gives you closure; you give it to yourself.

At that cafe, there was a massive poster of Bob Marley and his quote under it: 'The biggest coward of a man is to awaken the love of a woman without the intention of loving her.' I stared at the words for a while and then posted a picture of it on my gram. The first person to comment on it was Aman. He was guilty and replied to it saying, 'I never thought you wouldn't understand me.'

That's it. That's all I needed to snap out of everything I was feeling. His message was the turning point, the jolt I needed to awaken from my emotional stupor. He understood the gravity of his actions and his response only reaffirmed the weight of his guilt.

He wrecked my life. His words cut through the silence. He said, 'I thought you were the only person who would understand me. It was not as if I didn't want to love you. I couldn't comprehend what I wanted and gauge my feelings. When I needed you the most, you cut me out.'

He shamelessly played the victim, but his words reeked of narcissism as he said, 'I never intended to hurt you; I was merely lost and confused.' It was as though he believed his turmoil justified the pain he inflicted. His level of self-absorption left me astounded.

A man who had robbed me of countless nights of peace, the one who pushed me to the wall and caused me weeks of several panic attacks because he couldn't make a choice between two women, playing both sides and lying to everyone, especially me, was now taking the high moral ground and telling me I was being harsh. Harsh? It was my benevolence that he was let off the hook that easily. I was the victim here. I was heartbroken by his behaviour and I wouldn't stand for his nonsense any longer, let alone be lectured about how I should heal myself from something he broke.

I ghosted him, no regrets. He didn't deserve a single word from me.

Life, since the break-up, had been a routine of tears, panic attacks and insomnia. I had made my decision, but I still needed to emotionally disconnect. His response was that eureka moment where I realized who he really was—a narcissist, who when confronted, would play the victim. In that second, I blocked him for good. He deserved no place in my life, not then, not ever . . .

That night, I slept like a baby for the first time since Aman and I started seeing each other. Remember the gut feeling I told you about? I don't know why it kept me on the edge and awake for three months straight regardless of what good was happening in my life. It's almost as if my nervous system knew this was how it would turn out. That day, after haunting me for a while, my insomnia was magically fixed.

Now, I wanted to heal; I didn't want to be around our memories any more. My bouts of grief were worrying my parents and they, of all people, didn't deserve it!

The decision to leave Lucknow and start again in Delhi was like a breath of fresh air. It was daunting at first, leaving behind the city where I had my family, my loved ones, my entire social circle and those countless memories with Aman, but I knew it was the only way to truly move on.

It takes me a while to move on from something I love. But the beauty of my personality is that, once I have made up my mind, no one in the world can change it except me. This was a decision I had made. So now, even if Aman were to come begging to my doorstep or cry copious amounts of tears, he and I were over. I don't believe in second chances. When I am done, I am truly done!

The process of extracting myself from those familiar spaces was excruciatingly challenging. I left behind the cafes we used to visit, the streets we walked hand in hand and the places that held the echoes of our laughter. It was a clean break, a necessary severance from the past.

In Delhi, I would be surrounded by new faces and new places. I wanted to throw myself into my new job. The daily challenges would give me a sense of purpose.

I knew it wouldn't be an easy journey, but it was a necessary one. It would be an uphill task to let go of the anger, hurt and resentment, and focus on self-love.

But there was hope of rediscovering myself, my passions and my dreams.

Who knew that in Delhi, I would not only find a new job and a new city but also a new me, leaving the safety net behind to embrace the endless possibilities that life had in store? It did far more for me than I could have ever imagined. But not without a touch of drama . . . life enjoys throwing a little extra suspense in the plot, just to keep things interesting.

Mentally, I gave up on love. I never wanted to be vulnerable again in front of another person. I didn't want a romantic relationship in my life ever again. I wanted to be with myself. Love only caused pain and emotional wreckage. I wanted to be passive and less involved, and decided to not get into anything messy. I was only looking for professional laurels in the ruins of my heart. The doors to my soul were shut for good. There was a big lock dangling, with no key.

FROM AC'S DESK

In the 1997 movie *My Best Friend's Wedding*, Julia Roberts' character Julianne Potter says,

> Michael, I love you. I've loved you for nine years. I've just been too arrogant and scared to realize it, and, well, now, I'm just scared, so I realize this comes at a very inopportune time, but I really have this gigantic favour to ask of you. Choose me. M-marry me. Let me make you happy.

The scene beautifully captures the confusion in feelings and relationships at large. What we feel towards someone can ebb and flow like the sea, often leaving us conflicted.

Or in the brilliantly scripted 1989 film *When Harry Met Sally*, Harry says,

> Yes, that''s right, men and women can't be friends. Unless both of them are involved with other people, then they can. This is an amendment to the earlier rule.' If the two people are in a relationship, the pressure of possible involvement is lifted. That doesn't work either, because what happens then is the person you're involved with can't understand why you need to be

friends with the person you're just friends with. Like it means something is missing from the relationship and why do you have to go outside to get it? And when you say 'no, no, no it's not true, nothing is missing from the relationship', the person you're involved with then accuses you of being secretly attracted to the person you're just friends with, which you probably are. I mean, come on, who the hell are we kidding, let's face it. Which brings us back to the earlier rule before the amendment, which is 'men and women can't be friends'.

While movies at large have often romanticized the idea of best friends falling in love and given it mostly shades of purple hues and mushy doe-eyed finality, what happens to those friends whose already beautifully crafted relationship becomes marred with sensual overtures? What happens when friendships suffer after romance enters through the door? What happens to the friends when the lovers take over? Falling in love with the best friend can be a much bigger conundrum than depicted on celluloid.

When you know a person for long enough and have safety and comfort with them, the feelings transitioning into romantic or sexual life is a possibility. But what happens after that is often a labyrinth of complex emotions that two people must negotiate to preserve what they have or bomb it down completely.

What's important to remember is that we have no control on how we feel. But we have control over what we choose to do with the feelings. Greek Stoic Philosopher Epictetus talks about the gap or pause between the impetus and the response and believes that all our wisdom lies in that gap. So, whether to act out the feelings and transform the relationship, or to ingest, process and navigate those feelings and carry on, at the cost of being inauthentic or discuss it between the two friends and mutually give it a shape and form remains a choice. This very precarious choice often decides the fate of the relationship at large.

What's interesting is how we often refer to 'love between friends' as platonic. Rummaging through Western philosophy reveals that Plato (who the word is coined upon) believed that platonic love was a ladder on which love climbs up a series of steps to reach the peak of a 'a supreme idea'.[13] So, in a way, when two people can transcend the physical, sexual or sensual and go over to the higher ideas of love, it's termed platonic. We tend to casually

---

[13] Luis Ospino, 'Platonic Love: The Concept of Greek Philosopher Plato', Greek Reporter, 2 September 2023, https://greekreporter.com/2023/09/02/platonic-love-greek-philosopher-plato/.

use the word platonic to describe a kind of love that's devoid of sex, while the original meaning is where our minds and bodies have transcended all the other possibilities of how the relationship can shape up, and give it a more spiritual place . . .

Theory aside, the tragedy of love failing between best friends is that often the friendship suffers as well. The loss can be colossal. You lose two relationships and one whole person, who meant the world to you. Add to that, this person knows too much about you anyway, the way your mind works, what hurts you, your taste in music, your pet's favourite treat, your workplace chaos, your deep belly laugh and your past patterns. That makes the whole situation trickier. The best friend knows too much. Therefore, the internal turmoil, when love fails between two best friends, is far more complicated than a straightforward person-meets-person scenario.

So, what does one do? How does one even face such a loss? Who would have thought that the person closest to you would become a challenge? One thinks it's common sense, that the better we know someone, the more chances of things working out. But lo and behold, here we are, challenging our common sense.

Yeah, so what do I do with this potpourri of mixed feelings? First, it may be important to ask the question, 'What am I feeling?' Talking to a friend or a confidant, taking a small break from routine, reaching out to your support network and journaling for clarity, are often seen as important tools at this point. And the biggest thing you can do yourself when things are falling apart is to pause. Stop in your tracks, sit with yourself, breathe through it, cry it out, whatever you do, don't forget to pause. Our rush to sort out our pain often makes the wound deeper. So, give yourself grace and don't hurry to sort things out for yourself and between the both of you.

3

Light Your Own Cigarette

In the aftermath of my epic break-up saga, my tears took centre stage. Picture this: my eyes, typically the size of regular eyeballs, decided to channel the inner grief, swelling up as though training for the tear Olympics. In the weeks that followed, my eyes became overachievers, shedding liquid like a leaky faucet.

It felt like I had my rain cloud following me around, making sure I never forget my heartbreak. Nights became a one-person show of emotional acrobatics, with me perfecting the art of the silent sob. My pillow was humbly, unquestioningly soaking up the drama. My mirror had the dubious honour of witnessing my transformation into a mascara-ruined painting.

Okay, fear not, because, in this sap-filled sitcom, I was the hero in the making. The break-up blues were leading to a sequel which turned out to be way more uplifting. So, all the weeks and months of tears were a temporary setback for a permanent comeback. All delivered with a side of witty repartee and a sprinkle of sass.

The worst thing about those tears was that I had to cancel a lot of my shoots. My work was getting compromised because of my frequent emotional breakdowns after my break-up. But among those dark clouds was a silver lining. My Instagram following was soaring. In a month after my break-up, I had 100k followers, rather unexpectedly. I miraculously landed a job that would serve as my regular income. From my 2019 Mumbai stint, I had learnt that until my content career kicked off in full swing, some moonlighting would be good for my bank account and mental health. Not having a lump sum land in my account every month was something my heart didn't handle well. And given the already tattered condition it was in, it was best not to put any strain on myself. I was thus glad my ex-boss hired me for a show rather out of the blue.

On a bright January morning, I packed everything I could find within the reach of my hand and fled Lucknow. It was a desperate attempt to get away physically and find a space where I could grieve in peace. I had lost all faith in friendship and the love in my heart—for anybody. It's a strange place to be in. It felt like a vacuum—I was unmoved and empty.

Emotional desolation is a void that you create after a break-up. Connections are absent and the weight of solitude is all mixed. It is a peculiar emptiness. For me, it was an uncharted space where the usual currents of warmth and affection seemed to dissipate into nothingness. It was a place where my heart's love had retreated, leaving behind a sharp stillness that mirrored the unmoved state of my soul.

When I moved to Delhi, I called an old friend, Mridul, asking him for a favour—to stay with him until I could find a place of my own. I still remember, when I was making that call, I knew that even if he turned down my request, it wouldn't matter to me. But now when I look back, I realize that the world would cease to exist without the kindness of our friends who show up when we least expect them to. He asked me to just come over without another thought. At his home, I met another old friend of mine, Ishita, with whom I lived in 2015. It was a strange time. When I had made up my mind to remain emotionally aloof from everyone, the universe said to me, 'Dude, let's stick to my plan instead.'

Within days of getting there, I contracted Covid. It was the second wave of the pandemic. I was away from home and my family. I was with people who I had just reconnected with after seven years. My guards were up, and I knew I didn't want anyone to make their way in. But Ishita mothered me like I was her child. She made sure my meals were served to me on time. She would get the food made and leave it at the door. She monitored my temperature. She kept in touch with the doctor and made sure I had my medicines. For two weeks, she was on her toes. I was honestly surprised. Imagine the sorry situation. I was so emotionally scorched that even the simplest displays of basic humanity came as a genuine surprise. My bar was that low.

When my best friend of eight years, the love of my life, did what he did, how could I expect anyone else to do better?

I am glad I met Ishita in this phase of my life. She and I helped each other get past something that only we could see in each other. We were both broken differently and shattered in ways that needed healing. She was in a toxic relationship at that point, with some abuse, leading to gaslighting that caused her to blame herself. This was my trigger. I had routinely seen women make excuses for badly behaved men. Hell, a few weeks ago, I was doing the same for Aman. And I want to say it to all the sisters out there—you didn't drive him to the point where he was forced to slap you because he couldn't handle your temper. *IT IS NOT ON YOU!* I can't physically be there to shake you all up, but this is me virtually shaking you up with my words—you didn't cause it.

Ishita's pain made me cry. It was almost as if my feelings were returning; I was starting to care again. Something I had sworn off completely, was coming back to me naturally. I couldn't believe that good women like me, Ishita and so many of my friends were handed such bad cards in life. Why were people playing so dirty with us?

I knew I couldn't let Ishita face her turmoil alone. No one could be there for me, but I wanted to be there for her. In helping her leave a relationship that was eating her alive, I was able to put some balm on my wounds. I think we just lucked out. At a time in our lives, when we were down in the dumps, we found each other.

> *When it hasn't been your day, your week, your*
> *month, even your year . . .*
> *I'll be there for you . . .*[14]

I lost a Chandler but found myself a Joey for life. It's the sort of eternal love story that is about being each other's anchors and safe spaces. Who said soulmates need to be your lovers? Sometimes, it's your friends.

---

[14] The Rembrandts, 'I'll Be There for You', featured in *Friends* (1994–2004).

When the going gets impossible, I know Ishita, my twisted sister, will be there.

In the first few months in Delhi, I was lost. Amidst the ebb and flow of the bustling world, there are moments when one can't help but appear adrift in the vast sea of uncertainties. Furrowed brows and wandering eyes betrayed my mind; it was as if the soul had momentarily disconnected from its bearings. I was in a constant state of bewilderment. The lost gaze, searching for familiar feelings in unfamiliar terrain, was what I had become.

I had to keep my mind off Aman. I made myself a quick checklist, something I swore by. God forbid, if you are in the same place, try it:

1. Block them everywhere; they are dead to you.
2. Repeat point 1.
3. Mute those who try to mention them.
4. Sympathy is great but stop wallowing in self-pity.
5. The worst is over; get up and get going.
6. Your dreams are bigger than the boy who didn't deserve you.
7. Work Work Work Work.
8. Make a goal sheet and work towards them.

There is a reason why people seek professional gratification during personal lows. It's quick validation. It's so consuming that it distracts you. Work is also transactional and has limited scope to cause pain.

I wanted to evade the pain that had left me so brutally scarred. It was the sort of ache I didn't deserve. Overworking and under-feeling were beginning to make me selfish. I saw relationships in the same way I saw work. If you texted me once, I would text you once. If you sent me a compliment, I'd do the same. If you said something nasty, oh well, ditto, to you too!

From this rage emerged my alter ego—SoHarshi. You all know her by the Instagram handle. She is a bit of me and a lot of who I wanted to be at that point. She was slightly unhinged, unapologetically badass, full of righteous rage and intimidating. You wouldn't want to mess with this person. There is something about creating an alter ego that's an offshoot of our personality, but never quite authentically us. Shah Rukh Khan is on point when he says, 'I'm an employee of the myth of Shah Rukh Khan.'[15]

---

[15] 'Shah Rukh Khan is self-evasive on David Letterman's talk show: I tell everyone I am an employee of the myth of SRK', Firstpost, 25 October 2019, https://www.firstpost.com/entertainment/shah-rukh-khan-is-self-evasive-on-david-lettermans-talk-show-i-tell-everyone-i-am-an-employee-of-the-myth-of-srk-7555121.html.

I, too, got 'hired' by SoHarshi to build a persona of invincibility. You dare not mess with this girl.

But SoHarshi taught me something valuable, something most of us miss in our lives. She taught me that I am my priority. I learnt to say the most valuable word: No. I was a people pleaser before, but it was important to learn that you shouldn't feel the need to push your boundaries to accommodate anyone else. What people who promote these pristine ideas of self-sacrifice don't realize is that people who are in a bad place, are incapable of taking care of others. It's healthy to have boundaries. People who love you will understand you.

I had been in a space where I had fallen in love, literally. I had fallen in my own eyes. And I had a rule: don't question what anyone does in love. It's embarrassing, humiliating, heartbreaking and nerve-racking, but it's also just as integral to finding who you are and what you are made of.

Creating SoHarshi was me proving to myself that I am worth a million bucks. And imagine, if that's who I was in my worst of times, I knew that the best was yet to come.

Days in Delhi began to get better. Ishita fixed me. We would work out together and listen to Jagjit Singh together. We even downloaded Hinge together.

I was talking to her matches and she was to mine. Of course, neither of us was prepared to love again. But dating could be interesting.

(WRONG)

Not to dissuade anyone, but we girls have some horror stories to report.

Sample this: Ishita was chatting with a boy who called her the very second they started chatting. She wasn't ready for it and maybe she shouldn't have answered it. But she thought, how bad can a phone call be? Turns out a phone call can creep you out for life. The not-so-gentleman was masturbating on the other end. He was asking strange questions. We thought, why let him have all the fun? I told Ishita to keep the call going. It was barely minutes into the chat that the bloke on the other end was at the epitome of pleasure. But right before he could have his way, Ishita disconnected the call. We blocked him and reported it.

Yes, yuck! But that night, Ishita and I laughed like we hadn't in years.

Some stories, however, are far less humorous. I had always dated people who I knew. But in Delhi, I got a full dating app experience. I wouldn't diss it because many people find their great love story via technology. I just didn't get lucky.

There were weeks when I was mindlessly talking to men who were unable to hold my interest. Maybe I was broken. Maybe I was just off love, romance or the promise of a happily-ever-after. I would chat for two or three days, then get bored of answering the same questions—oh, where are you from? How come you are on the app? The rigmarole of it was draining. By day three, with each of them, I had this strong urge to shut down. After a point, I lost count of the number of people I was ghosting.

I met some interesting people too. I connected with this lawyer who came from a farming background. Every weekend, he would be at his farm. Sometimes he'd send pictures of his buffaloes. I was finding it adorable until the point I realized there was no chemistry. Now that I had been with someone who knew my silences, I had an unnatural expectation of the same from everyone without noting the fact that I wasn't investing enough to create that.

There was another man I found charming, but he was too broken to be in anything. He didn't believe in healing or therapy. I knew after the first call, most of which he spent talking about his ex, that this would go south. My only takeaway was that most people don't believe in healing after a break-up. One broken person carries all their pain and dumps it on their next, in the process breaking them too.

How do you heal? I thought by finding someone evolved, kind and more sorted than who I had been with.

And then something happened. I met somebody who seemed like the one I was looking for. Let's talk about him. He was an entrepreneur from Canada.

Because it was around the pandemic, I invited him home. It was the first hinge date of my life. I had a flatmate at home, so we weren't technically alone. He was a regular boy next door. Kind, funny, wonderful. He brought a bottle of wine. We kissed that night after hours of chatting and laughing together. He tried to go further but I stopped him saying I wasn't comfortable. He respected my boundaries and backed off. We went back to bantering, doing bhangra on Hindi songs. At some point, he asked, 'Why was I single?' By the time you are in your late twenties, you usually have had one relationship that didn't work out. It is a common question. But I wasn't ready to answer it. I looked at him, tried to find words and burst into tears. I am grateful to him for his kindness that night. He handled me with care and caressed my head as I cried myself to sleep. When I woke up later that night, he was gone. I am not sure if it was the alcohol, his warmth or the pain in my heart, but clearly I was not healed from my past. I apologized to him the next day and he was rather sweet about it.

I should have put the brakes on my dating life at this point, but I somehow ended up going on a date with another man. The first time we met, it was for a long drive. He and I knew very well that it could, at best, be a summer fling. But we wanted to meet again. Perhaps there could be more. I thought 'let's give it a shot at least'. In keeping with my spontaneous streak, I was like—what's the worst that can happen? It won't work out. Okay.

Turns out a date can easily become a freak show. This was the sort of bad date that could've gone down in the annals of dating infamy. Instead of going out, we met at my place because lockdown restrictions were still in effect. He was normal at first. We chatted over pizzas. We drank a bit. He kissed me. He wanted to go further, but when I stopped him saying I wasn't okay with going further. But not all men understand the concept of 'No'. He slapped me twice, very hard. My brain froze. I wanted to scream and call for Ishita who was in the next room. But my body froze, I didn't know what to do.

I had been talking to the guy on the app for five months before we met. We had chatted over calls before we met. He wasn't a random stranger I picked up. I thought I knew him.

But then he went on to do something unimaginable. He molested me. That's when I broke down. He was shocked and it was like he broke out of some kinky dream he was trying to live. He zipped himself up and said sorry. But I was too scared to react. I asked him to leave. He apologized and left.

It took me a few minutes to gain composure. I ran to Ishita, who was puzzled to see my condition. There were finger marks on my face. I had a narrow escape from the clutches of a psychopath. That night, I slept in Ishita's room.

The next day, I uninstalled Hinge. This wasn't for me. Moreover, I needed to heal.

Within a month of coming to Delhi, I left the safety net of the job. I was approached by a management agency that signed me up as an artist. I became a freelancer and started getting regular work. My career became a focus during my first year in Delhi. People don't realize how challenging freelance life can be. If you don't have a routine, you cannot do it. I put myself into order, knowing very well that the opportunity to scale up wouldn't come again. I wanted to work hard for my dream.

I would wake up in the morning as the first rays of dawn filtered through my curtains, casting a warm glow upon my room. This was a space I made for myself from scratch. I stretched beneath the comforting cocoon of sheets, relishing the quietude that lingered in the air. But I didn't give myself enough time to enjoy the morning. It was time to hustle already.

I would rise from my bed and approach the window, drawn to the promise of a new day.

In my kitchen, I would whip up a storm. Breakfast was an affair coupled with the rich, aromatic overture of chai. The scent would waft through the air, enveloping me in a cosy cocoon as I savoured each sip while perched by the window. I would listen to Taylor Swift songs and feed myself a big breakfast with toast, avocado and scrambled eggs.

Cause the players gonna play, play, play, play, play
And the haters gonna hate, hate, hate, hate, hate
Baby, I'm just gonna shake, shake, shake, shake, shake
I shake it off, I shake it off . . .[16]

Mindfulness was a sacred ritual, be it as a pause in time for meditation or turning the pages of a book. My 'me time' had become sacrosanct.

I was very sincere about my workouts. As someone who has battled weight issues, I would never miss a day of working out. Ishita was a brilliant workout partner. She was in the phase where she wanted to shed a few pounds. We would work out together, eat clean and listen to music every morning.

Once the lockdown restrictions were over, she went back to work. I would set up my makeshift office in the living room. By evening, I would take a long bubble bath. Put some scented candles in the room. Ishita and I would have soup together and talk about our respective days. Then we would drift off to sleep, huddled together.

---

[16] Taylor Swift, 'Shake it off' (2014).

The whole process was therapeutic for me. And I found my way to words. I wrote with the sort of authenticity I never had before. The highs and lows of life created a deeply relatable and cathartic experience for the audience and that's what I put into my content. Navigating the intricacies of love, heartbreak and self-discovery, I developed content that was a poignant reflection of the human experience.

Most days, my content-creator friends would come over. You all know Sanyam Sharma and Yuvraj Dua by their names. They are indeed the most joyous collaborators to work with. We would sometimes brainstorm together and come up with concept videos. Some days, I would work alone and write for many hours at a stretch.

Working with them made me realize that candid storytelling is important to grow as an artist. Take your pain and make art with it. And that's how we came up with the *Bestfriend* series. I held on to the good from my time with Aman and let go of the bad. With Sanyam, I started the series that busted the idea that 'ek ladka aur ladki kabhi ache dost nahi ho saktey'.

The validation we got for it was unparalleled. People loved it. This is when our views began to skyrocket. The numbers were unimaginable, starting with thousands and very soon touching millions and more.

Success has a transformative quality, often filling your life with optimism and more.

We were seeing the anthemic nature of our work and our followers were soaring. Yuvraj and I started the *Movie Character* series, and we were filled with empowering messages from fans. I solely credit this love to the unbelievable ability artists possess to turn personal narratives into universal stories. This is what contributes to the enduring impact of our work, creating a space where people can find solace, empowerment and a sense of belonging.

Over time, these content creator friends I was working with became my closest friends, and eventually, like family. In the hustle and bustle of work, we got to know each other—our ups, downs and everything in between.

In the small moments of each day, they ended up becoming more than just coworkers. We were there for each other through thick and thin. In the busy and sometimes stressful work life, we became partners in crimes and cheerleaders in good times. They say competition is about wanting to pull each other down; I am thankful I found a tribe that only believed in pushing each other up.

Strangely enough, I wasn't looking for a man any more. After the semi-scarring date and a doomed relationship before that, I wanted to stop piercing myself with the shards of my broken heart. I wasn't looking for anyone or anything. I was living in the moment, enjoying the little joys of everyday life. Embracing solitude made me delve into the depths of my own emotions. I discovered the art of celebrating myself.

I was happily single. I had never been single in my life until this point. I had always been in long-term relationships. There was always a man waiting for me at the end of the day, who'd ask me how it went.

Embracing the new-found solitude, I found comfort in the quiet moments that were previously drowned out by the constant hum of companionship. The stillness of my own company became a safe haven, allowing me to rediscover the intricacies of my individuality that had been somewhat obscured so far.

Singlehood made me realize that my world wasn't defined solely by the presence of someone else. Instead, it opened a space where I could explore my desires, dreams and aspirations.

Without the tether of a committed relationship, I had the opportunity to explore new facets of my identity, to indulge in hobbies that had long been relegated to the background, and to forge connections with myself that were deeper and more introspective. The evenings were no longer punctuated by the familiar inquiry of a partner asking what I wanted to do with them. I was the master of my time; I could do whatever I wanted.

The quiet of the solitary existence began to echo with the laughter of new-found friendships. I reveled in the spontaneity of my own choices, relishing the freedom to chart my course without compromise. It wasn't a rejection of companionship, but rather a celebration of independence that allowed me to redefine my priorities.

In this chapter of my life, the absence of a constant companion did not equate to loneliness; instead, it paved the way for a profound connection with the person I was becoming. Each day unfolded as a blank page, ready to be filled with the stories, adventures and personal triumphs that were just mine.

As the days turned into weeks and weeks into months, I found that being happily single wasn't just a transient state but a conscious choice. The question of 'how did it go' at the end of the day became an internal dialogue.

This space that life had granted me was for me to find out who I am. I met Harshita in all her pain and glory. She was a standout girl who didn't give herself enough credit.

> *I'll be there for you*
> *(When the rain starts to pour)*
> *I'll be there for you*
> *(Like I've been there before)*
> *I'll be there for you*

Oh well, guys. *Friends* forgot to tell us—it's as important to be there for yourself!
Kaan kholo aur padho. (Open your ears and read.)

Here's a checklist on how to move on:

1. Stop staring at his WhatsApp DP. He isn't that cute. Block his number. Then delete his number. A clean cut would be the best.
2. Stop talking about them. Stop taking their name. You don't have to tell stories about them. Forget they ever existed!
3. Unfollow him on Instagram. Don't block him. Let him see you having a ball of a time in a few months. Because you will.
4. Mute everyone around you who brings him up. You don't need to know *babu ne khana khaya ki nahi*! (Did my baby eat their food?)
5. Donate all the gifts you have gathered from the relationship. You deserve good karma points.
6. All the items you've stolen from your partner—shirts, shorts, moisturizers, mugs, books—can be donated too. #JustSaying
7. Delete all chats. You don't need to know what went wrong. The rest, your therapist will help you figure out.
8. Find new addas. Stop visiting old places.
9. Those friends who you put on the bench for this relationship, reconnect with them. And start with a sorry.
10. Look like the bombshell you are. And find your own version of the revenge dress.

11. Light your own cigarette; well, that's also our
next chapter and 'Oh My God' (in the most
Janice voice), the hardest part of moving on.

Love has a funny way of sneaking up on you when
you least expect it. It's waiting in the shadows until
you've got your guard down. And when you focus on
embracing the wonderful person you are, that's when
love decides to make a grand entrance, sweeping you
off your feet most unexpectedly and delightfully. It's
like the universe saying, 'Hey, you've done the work,
now enjoy the sweet reward . . . '

And my sweet reward was just round the corner.
Eight months later, I met the man of my dreams . . .

FROM AC'S DESK

The mess during the transition phase, as the nature of our relationships begins to change, is often marked by a concoction of blocking, unblocking, stalking, hacking (passwords), panicking, screaming, shouting and crying. The best-friend heartbreak is nothing less than a mess because the person was not just close to us but to our family, friends and social settings. They were part of our family albums. What a bizarre mess. The proximity just makes it too hard to comprehend what to do next.

The mess is just uncertainty. The jumbled wires of our life that we must painstakingly now untangle; all the while hoping it all goes away. But it does not. Because as we try to undo, un-say and untangle things, the messier it all continues to become.

This stage is required. Uncertainty and confusion are required. It's an important stage in the heartbreak journey. They are the clouds before the rain. And there is no running away from it. Uncertainty is our limited knowledge and lack of control over the situation. It's having no plan and naturally, can be very distressing. And this distress has no quick fixes. While this phase may be filled with all kinds of disturbing emotions, it's one of the more positive phases, because from falling apart, will come change.

It's a stressful period for sure. You may be too keen to rebuild what's broken, you may plead with your friend, you may one day hate him and by evening want him back in your life. While the phase feels chaotic and you are running pillar to post to just bring in some normalcy, remind yourself that this is a phase, and it will pass. It will feel like a never-ending tunnel, but there is light at the other end of the messy period. Interestingly, you will be most reactive in this phase. Trying to change the course of your life, wrestling with the truth, getting agitated with reality. It's common, uncertainty tends to put us in the fight and flight mode. And in the state, our reactivity is at its highest.

Few ways to calm your fight-or-flight response:

1. Deep breathing
2. Psychological sighs
3. Positive affirmations
4. Moving your body
5. Mantra chanting
6. Butterfly taps
7. Hugging yourself
8. Humming
9. Gargling
10. Using a weighted blanket

As we work on composing ourselves and go through our anger, pain, sense of betrayal and hopelessness, we will discover grief. We sometimes lose people to life, not just to death. As John Green in *The Fault in Our Stars* says, 'Grief doesn't change you, it reveals you'.[17]

While anger and pain are often the primary emotions before we can move to the other stages in such a case, taking time to grieve is paramount. Losing a friend and a partner, all at once, is going through all stages of grief. And going through all the stages of grief—denial, anger, bargaining, depression and finally at some point, acceptance—is important.

It is crucial to mention here that heartbreak takes time to heal, and while we may be tempted to jump back into the dating scene to use it as a band-aid to our hurt, it's best to rein ourselves in at this point. During such times, one tends to rush into dating often as a means to soothe themselves, but it's actually a critical time to invest in oneself emotionally. The processing of confusing and conflicting emotions at this point is the most important work.

---

[17] John Green, *The Fault in Our Stars* (UK: Penguin, 2012).

4

Unicorn *ki Talaash*[18]

It's interesting that I am writing this today. It's Diwali of 2023. I sit at home with my beautiful dog Coco, persuading him to finish his meal. The house is shimmering like a beautifully bejewelled new bride. And it ought to, right? This is my last Diwali at home before I get married in two weeks. It's only fitting that it look like a sight to behold.

It's a little crazy that I am thinking of the days spent breaking down at this very home. I mean why, on a good day, would I think of that? Because the good times can never come to you without the hurt of the bad ones.

It's taken a lot of healing to make it to this place. I have been shattered and put back together a few times and I know life will continue to wring me now and then. But I consciously never want to forget

---

[18] The search for the unicorn.

my bad times; they remind me of everything that followed.

So tonight, hiding my face in Coco's fur, I decide to write a letter to everyone who is breaking apart right now . . .

Dear You,

I am sorry you are going through so much. I want you to know I have been there too. There were mornings after mornings when I would wake up and simply burst into tears. The pain in my heart would make my chest hurt. I couldn't function, I couldn't move. I would quietly stare at the wall, a million thoughts in my mind.

I know when one is in the middle of it, it feels lonely. Like why is this happening to me? What bad have I done to deserve this? I want to let you know—yes, you are a good person. No, it's not some karma biting you back. Stop saying that to yourself. Put some logic to it—do you feel it's karma when something bad happens to a kid? No, right. Then, how can this be created by karma?

There is a museum in Croatia—the Museum of Broken Relationships, where people leave the things their partners left with them. It helps them move on. This tribe of those who've been heartbroken—we are innumerable, we are strong and, above all, we are healing every day.

I had read somewhere about how grief is not something that goes away. Truly, it doesn't. It stays with you. It lingers and follows you, and eventually, you work through it. If you close your eyes, it might transport you back to exactly where you were. It's palpable. But over time, you make space for your life amidst all the grief. When the love of people around you fills your life, the grief looks a lot less consuming. Like a speck, almost not there. It might be within the reach of your fingers, but you don't get to it.

The weight of lost love bores down on your shoulders, and you doubt if happiness will ever find its way back into your life. In those moments, it feels like the sun has set for good. I wish I could reach through and hold you close, whispering that the ache will eventually fade.

I am afraid you have to carry your broken heart. There is no fixing it. But what it does is that you can see the cracks in someone else's heart. It makes you kinder, more empathetic and even more sensitive if possible. (I am not talking of the fuckboys though; they'd find some other reason to fuck around if it wasn't about being cheated upon).

I have come to realize that heartbreaks are some sort of magical pathway that takes us to something that we didn't know existed in us—our ability to feel. Would you be living if you didn't feel? A closed heart is an unused heart, and you were put on earth to live after all. Break open that heart and live with abandon.

I want you to know that the journey of healing is tumultuous, and though you may not believe it now, the heartbreak that you so loathe right now will shape you in ways unimaginable.

I am standing on the brink of a new phase of life. And someday, you'll be here too. That day, I want you to look back and appreciate the strength you found amid your deepest sorrows. You emerged from that darkness with a resilience that will astonish you. The scars you carry are not blemishes but markers of your journey.

Love will find you again in the most unexpected of places and in the most unexpected of ways. The love you once thought irreplaceable was but a prelude to the epic romance that awaits you. It is not an instant fix; it is a gradual mending of the fragments of your heart. In the arms of another, you will discover a love that will be patient, kind and utterly transformative. I hate the term being 'mad in love', but someday you'll value being calm in love. Don't be afraid to love wholeheartedly, for in vulnerability lies the essence of true connection.

I won't sugarcoat it—there will be many bad days before you get there and many more even after that. Happiness, romance, none of it is absolute. There will be moments when you question if you have the strength to weather the storms. But remember, that your heartbreaks will make you someone capable of embracing the beauty that arises from the ashes of pain.

As I take the steps down the aisle, I will remember the journey to that moment was as important as the destination.

You too, cherish every step, every stumble, and every leap of faith. I pray that someday you too find love again and make it where I am. It is a triumph over the past, and proof of the resilience of the human heart.

Bharosa rakho, pyaar milega . . . (Keep faith, you'll find love . . .)

Geeli Puchi,[19]
HG

Now, at the end of the last chapter, I told you to light your own cigarette. Since you've followed Aman and my story beat by beat, you know what I meant. One of the most important shifts I had to make after my break-up was to start lighting my cigarette. Sounds innocuous, right? Well, maybe, but imagine being in a relationship for years and

---

[19] Wet kisses.

years. It becomes second nature, almost like a habit. I still remember the first cigarette after my split with Aman. I had never carried my own lighter till that point. I was flustered looking for a light and then made a mental note—carry your own lighter, woman! But some habits had to change.

One of the hardest things to do in those days was to avoid getting into a rebound relationship. When Dr Callie Torres in Season 4 of *Grey's Anatomy* says, 'You didn't love her! You just didn't want to be alone. Or maybe, maybe she was good for your ego. Or, or maybe she made you feel better about your miserable life, but you didn't love her, because you don't destroy the person that you love,' I felt her. Seeing her being shattered bit by bit by the man she married filled me with pain. How could George do that to her? How could she be so blind in love to not see it? But then again, my fundamental rule is—never judge someone who is in love. They will fuck up a lot, and go really deep and far to make it work.

But even when I broke up with Aman, I knew I wasn't cut out for a quick rebound. I didn't want to manipulate someone into believing I love him. I wasn't in the condition to love myself; another person was a much later story. Rebound relationships are the most painful to witness. You take someone on a ride because you are in too much pain and can do with a quick balm on your heart. It's good for your soul to feel validated. But then the person begins to invest and fall for you, and you fuck the person up. If you want a shoulder to cry on, find friends and a therapist. If you decide on a rebound, always be honest about it to the other person. Make sure they are ok with, knowing that it's a rebound situation. Some people can emotionally detach.

I, on the other hand, believed in happily-ever-afters. I was always certain I wanted to get married ever since I was a little girl. I came from a middle-class home in Lucknow where the idea of marriage just seeps into your system very early on. Growing up, I was devoid of ambition. Today, when people see me planning my life around work, they are pleasantly surprised. I was never this person. But post the break-up, I threw myself neck deep into work.

Back then, with the two terrible tech-love experiences, I realized it is not easy to exist in this modern dating pool where romance is viewed as transient, and people have the burning desire to hop from one to the other. After Aman, I wasn't prepared to be shaken up again the way I was. I didn't want to break down the way I did, all over again.

A few months after my break-up, I told my parents to find me suitable suitors for marriage. I handed them an exhaustive list. It was a running joke that I was looking for a unicorn. I thought I had standards—they behaved like Sima Aunty from *Indian Matchmaking,* saying, 'You won't get a 100 per cent match; if 60–70 per cent of your criteria are met, you should proceed . . . '

But I wouldn't budge. I knew I was looking for someone who'd fit me like a glove. He'd be perfect for me. Someone charming, good-looking, who held a respectable job, loved my family, respected me, empowered me and fueled my ambition. My father told me, 'This boy doesn't exist. You need to lower the bar.' I was fine with not marrying perhaps, but coming down on what I was seeking was a no-go.

Exasperated, my father registered me on a matrimonial site. He paid them handsomely and got me a personalized Sima Aunty-like manager. Some of the suitors that came were not bad, but the filter was that of caste and money. My heart was still looking for love. What irked me a lot were the questions that came my way—do you want to live in a flat or bungalow? How much do you want your partner to earn—5 lakhs per month or 10 lakhs per month? When I told my father, he was stumped too.

It all felt too shallow. I wasn't attracted to anyone, physically or emotionally. So, while suitor profiles screened by my family and relationship manager, poured in by the bulk, I wasn't quite finding who I was looking for.

'Keep calm, everyone. There are pink fluffy unicorns dancing on the rainbows'.[20]

It. Will. Happen.

Someone had told me that for one to accept love, you have to open your heart. Mine had closed. It was shut. Initially, I knew it was me setting boundaries, but then slowly I realized, it was more. I was scared to freefall again.

There is nothing called a mutual break-up. One person initiates it, another merely agrees. In my case, though I had taken the stand on this, it was harder for me to move on. Before you move on, you need to heal your heart. I didn't want to make my next relationship dirty. I had rolled in the mud it was therapy that cleansed me.

A lot of people think therapy is a magic wand. But, life isn't a magical world where a few spells can magically fix everything. When we fall and hurt ourselves, we run to a doctor. The doctor cleans the wound, puts the needed medicines and balms, and gives us a painkiller. Depending on the depth of the wound, it takes just that much longer to heal. But when we wound our hearts, we don't give it enough

---

[20] Andrew Huang, 'Pink Fluffy Unicorns Dancing on Rainbows', 11 November 2010, https://www.youtube.com/watch?v=eWM2joNb9NE.

time to bounce back. Every medicine has its course; therapy works just like that.

Go for that first session. And then for the second, third and fourth. Give it time to work. The first pill can never fix you now, can it? If someone has busted their kneecap, it will take three months to get better. If your heart has shattered, you need to give it the time it needs. The thing about the human heart is that it can take a few days, weeks, months, years or even a lifetime to heal. The beauty of it, though, is that you somehow figure out a way of living through the pain. And over time it gets less and a lot easier.

Interestingly, my first tryst with depression was in 2016. It was caused by a toxic workplace and a bad manager. The entire generation of senior managers who believe it's alright to humiliate people into keeping them in line, have a special place in hell. I don't get jobs where embarrassing a young person is seen as pushing them to shine. Whoever came up with this is an idiot. Doesn't it sound like an oxymoron; almost like, I will clip the bird's wings to make it fly . . .

That's the long and short of what started it for me. And ever since, depression makes a comeback every few years to pull the rug from beneath my feet.

Everyone has symptoms; I can list out mine:

1. Weight loss: 8–9 kilos
2. Lack of drive or energy

3. Loss of appetite
4. Insomnia
5. Withdrawal from people
6. Cramps and headaches

The second time I realized I might be depressed was when I burst into tears one morning right before I was going to go on air for my morning show during my radio days. My ex-boss received a call from me while I was wailing on the other end.

At this time, I was already in therapy. But evidently, it wasn't working for me.

Do you know why? Because therapy, much like a marriage or relationship, is about finding the right fit. Some pearls of wisdom for my friends out there— don't give up therapy if it isn't working; chances are you need a different therapist who gets you better. That doctor wasn't meant for me, and I met many new therapists before I found my therapist.

And then I remember talking to her. She was that one hour of my day when I was at my most peaceful best.

Within the haven of my therapist's words, I uncovered a profound sense of hope that gently cradled my struggles. Her conviction assured me that within the tumult of my pain, lies an inherent strength. In those vulnerable moments, her words became a lifeline, affirming, 'You've got the power to heal.' It wasn't just a platitude; it felt like a revelation. 'It will get better,' she insisted, every few days. I felt heard, I felt someone was present for me, someone gets me.

She was right, I did possess the innate ability to rewrite my narrative to emerge from the shadows of pain into a brighter world and create a whole new version of myself.

But that's another thing about moving on. It's like a switch in your heart. You must want it actively and work towards it to get better. No shrink can help you if you don't decide for yourself. It's difficult to find the will to do this.

Tumhe khud hi apne dil ka move on switch on karna hoga . . . (You'll have to switch on the move-on button for your own heart . . .)

Say it aloud—I DESERVE BETTER IN LIFE.

From that moment on, things get better.

Here's a list of things you can tell yourself:

1. I am worthy of happiness
   Recognize that happiness is not a privilege; it's your birthright. Embrace it as you would a cherished gift, acknowledging your inherent worthiness.
2. My past does not define me
   Every tomorrow is a new page, untainted by yesterday's struggles. Your past is a chapter, not the whole story. Define yourself by the strength you embody today.

3. I choose positivity and optimism
   In every challenge, find an opportunity.
   Your mindset shapes your reality and by
   choosing positivity, you attract the energy of
   transformation.
4. I am resilient and strong
   Like a mighty oak weathering storms, you
   stand resilient. Each challenge you face is a
   show of your strength. You are not broken;
   you are a survivor.
5. I embrace change as a catalyst for growth
   Change is the sculptor of the masterpiece
   that is life. Embrace it, for in change lies
   the potential for growth, learning and the
   discovery of new, beautiful aspects of yourself.
6. I release what no longer serves me
   Just as a bird lets go of a branch to soar,
   release anything that weighs you down—be it
   past regrets, self-doubt or toxic relationships.
   Free yourself to fly.
7. I am the architect of my destiny
   Design a future that resonates with your
   dreams, ambitions and the love you deserve.
8. I attract positivity and abundance
   The energy you emit attracts like-minded
   forces. By radiating positivity, you draw
   abundance into your life—an abundance of
   love, opportunities and joy.

9. I am in control of my happiness

   Happiness is not dependent on external circumstances. It is a state of being cultivated from within. Take charge of your joy and let it radiate, illuminating the path to a brighter future.

10. (And most importantly) Stop resisting therapy

    Stop saying things like, 'she isn't saying anything new. I already know all the balderdash she is charging me for.' No, you don't. When you talk to them, you introspect. There is a lot of awareness while talking. You knew it for sure, but you realize it's not too late to change. Yes, you knew the red flags, but you chose to ignore them. The weight of love is now gone, and that red flag is the heaviest thing you are carrying. You need help shedding it.

P.S. You don't know better than the doctor. If you believe the doctor when he hands out antibiotics for a cough, believe the techniques your shrink is showing you. They work!

The flip side of this is that you start thinking your therapist is godlike. No, they aren't. They are just human. Every therapist needs a therapist too. Stop burdening them; respect their boundaries too.

They don't have spells. Stop calling them after their work hours. Bombarding them with calls at 11 p.m. from your bathroom floor is a terrible idea. Make that appointment for tomorrow.

My notes for you:

1. Find that will to get better.
2. Find the right therapist who makes you feel heard. You'll know when you find them.
3. Follow what your therapist says.

There is a lot of judgement around therapy. Sometimes, it takes you a while to come to terms with where you are in life. I didn't dare to tell people about my therapist for years. I am the closest to my father and even he didn't know about it. I told him only when I started getting better. And he said something kind, 'Do whatever you think is good for you. You always have me standing by your side.'

My father had seen me debilitated a few times in the past. I wouldn't smile for months; I wouldn't have the energy to shower; I would go from plump to lanky all of a sudden.

When I told him about my troubles during a light conversation on our terrace, he didn't react immediately. I fully acknowledged that they didn't get it. Their whole generation doesn't understand the idea of mental health, so it was surreal that he backed me. 'If you feel therapy is working, keep at it,' he told me.

Not judging me was the best thing he could have done for me. But I acknowledge that not everyone has supportive families and friends.

And here's my golden rule—you don't need to tell them about it. Do it in private. Tell them it's a work meeting. Make an excuse. Don't you lie about sneaking out with your girlfriend or boyfriend? There's no guilt when you do that. Then why do you not want to sneak out for something that you desperately need? Like your parents sometimes don't get your love, they might sometimes hold you back from loving yourself too. Make peace with it and do what's best for you.

For me too, therapy didn't work for months. I continued to be confused if I should fight for my love or let it all go. *Ye sabse ghatiya phase hota hai* (this is the worst phase of it all), TRUST ME.

But then, it took one sentence to turn it around. Three words actually: I AM DONE. And this time, *dil se*[21] . . . You can feel the snap in your heart.

Once I said the three words to Aman, everything worked out—my relationship, my love, my job, a new city, a home full of warm friends and a future brimming with unexplored possibilities.

---

[21] From the heart.

Not because I finally let go of Aman. But because I decided I deserved better, and I stuck by it. I am worthy of abundance and well, anything mediocre, just wouldn't cut it for me.

Oh, darling, call it what you want—selfish, self-centred or just downright fabulous—I chose myself over everything else because I am the designer of my happiness. If they think it's selfish to prioritize my joy, well then, let them swim in their sea of opinions while I bask in the glory of self-love. Who needs approval when you've got confidence sparkling brighter than their judgement?

Let's go back to where we began. Rebounds. I had tried it and, like I told you before, it didn't go very well.

I have had some distance to speak objectively about why I feel one should stay off rebounds:

1. Emotional healing: After a break-up, it's important to take time for self-discovery. Jumping into a new relationship too quickly may hinder the process of understanding and learning from the previous one.
2. Unresolved issues: Rebound relationships often occur before individuals have had

the chance to resolve the issues from their previous relationship. This can lead to carrying emotional baggage into the new relationship, which may create difficulties in the long run.

3. Comparisons and expectations: People in rebound relationships may compare their new partner to their ex, setting up unrealistic expectations or causing unnecessary stress. It's essential to enter a new relationship with an open mind and a fresh perspective.

4. Potential for regret: If someone enters a new relationship on a rebound, they might later realize that their feelings were influenced by the emotional aftermath of their previous relationship rather than genuine connection and compatibility with the new partner. This can lead to regret.

5. Risk of hurting others: Rebound relationships can inadvertently hurt the new partner, especially if they are more emotionally invested or expecting a more serious commitment than the person on the rebound is ready for.

6. Incomplete introspection: Taking time between relationships allows for introspection and personal growth. Engaging in a rebound relationship may delay this process, potentially leading to repeating patterns of

behaviour that contributed to the end of the previous relationship.

7. Never a substitute for closure: Some mistakenly believe that starting a new relationship will provide the closure they need. Closure typically comes from internal processes rather than external relationships.

During my post-break-up phase, I was frequently told that to get over a man, you should get under a man. It's the worst advice ever. Do not follow it. This notion that mindless sex can save you is bizarre. Have casual sex if you deem fit but do it because you want to have fun and not because it's a tape for your broken heart.

No spouse or partner can heal you from something someone else did to you. It's your battle. You'll have to fight it alone. And your therapist will give you a lot of ammunition to go to war, but it's a duel that's on you.

In the messy aftermath of a break-up, when it feels like love played a cruel trick on you, it's normal to want to throw in the towel. The fear of another heartbreak looms large and trusting love again seems like an open invitation for trouble. Think of it like a job interview—if you get turned down, do you not try for another job? Do you stay home and be unemployed for the rest of your lives?

But hey, hold up a second. Life's no fairy godmother with promises and guarantees, I get that.

Still, I've got a little nugget of wisdom for you: even if your heart pulls a Houdini act a million times, life has a funny way of sneaking in unexpectedly. There's a romcom in the next chapter; wait for it.

Think of it like this: love might be a wild roller coaster, but you are the badass rider who faces the twists and turns head-on. So, chin up, my friend. Life has got more surprises up its sleeve, and you are ready for them all.

It takes strength to love again, to put yourself out there, running the risk of being dismantled. It's beautiful to do that.

Love is not a person; it's a feeling. Karan Johar also lied about another thing: '*Hum ek baar jeete hai, ek baar marte hai aur pyar ek baar hi hota hai.*' (We live once, we die once and love happens only once.)[22] Love happens again and again. I have been in love thrice, and each experience has taught me so much about living. Do you want to know how? Because I stopped looking for my exes in people. Don't look for your past in your future. Give your new love a chance.

Don't compare new people with those in your past because what you had for seven years cannot be recreated in seven months. That doesn't mean what you have at hand is any less wonderful. Give that a chance, give yourself a chance. I have a solid reason why. Can you deny that there was something

---

[22] *Kuch Kuch Hota Hai* (1998).

awry and thus, your past relationship didn't work? They chose to let it go. You chose to let it go. Hold on to the lessons meant to be learnt and memories worth keeping.

And that brings me to my most crucial learning from heartbreak—in order to love right, you must love yourself first. Do you remember Carrie Bradshaw's last line in *Sex and the City* (1998–2004): 'The most exciting, challenging, and significant relationship of all is the one you have with yourself. And if you find someone to love the you that you love, well, that's just fabulous.'

And after some looking, I found the one who will love the moody, mercurial, wacko me. A fabulous love story, coming up! Turn the page . . .

(An actual picture of what the man of my dreams was expected to look like, and the reality came pretty close)

FROM AC'S DESK

Some mental health professionals write prescriptions; I get my patients to draw, paint, dance and doodle. These expressive arts modalities often prove to be very effective when we are trying to process our feelings and work on our healing. There are rules, sure, but nothing summarizes my opinion on the last chapter you read better than this doodle . . .

5

Un-Fuck Yourself

I am going to say something very controversial. The woke world doesn't allow you candour, but I just have to spell out what is pretty obvious about the dating world today. Poo in *Kabhi Khushi Kabhie Gham . . .* (2001) said it before me, 'Good looks, good looks, good looks.' Yes, she said it. It is an important facet for attracting someone that might potentially become the next big love of your life.

Don't dating apps remind you of your Amazon cart? You go window shopping when bored, now and then, add a few people to the cart and then purchase when someone catches your interest. Yes, dating apps often perpetuate a culture of superficiality, where individuals make snap judgements based primarily on physical appearance rather than genuine connection or compatibility.

Being attracted to George Clooney is natural, but I am not sure if one can date him or fall in love with him. Attraction or good looks could be the starting point but meaningful qualities such as personality, values and interests cannot take a backseat for very long. The allure of aesthetically pleasing images eventually passes and what matters is the comfort of that hug.

I guess I was looking for the one whose hug would make my heart feel—I am home.

Within seven months of living in the big city, I had decided to go full fortress mode, complete with a 'no entry' sign on my heart. Just when the world was coming out of lockdown, I had implemented a strict policy of emotional lockdown. So, until further notice, my heart had closed for renovations and the only guest allowed was me and my playlist of Taylor Swift's sassy empowerment anthems.

But then one day, it was just an ordinary day—or so I thought. Little did I know that a twist of fate awaited me, and my heart would take an unexpected turn. Love, it seems, has a way of finding us when we least expect it.

As I went about my days, the last thing on my mind was the possibility of finding someone. But life had other plans for me. A chance encounter, a shared smile, and suddenly, the world felt different. The emotions swirling within me were like a roller coaster—excitement, joy, and some anxiety. Wait . . . a lot of anxiety. How did this happen?

I was at a shoot in a godforsaken place on the outskirts of Manesar. There was nothing around for several kilometres. It was the day before Diwali and the idea was to finish work and take a flight home. I had just one line in a commercial we were shooting and had agreed to do it as the last gig before taking a holiday break.

You know, it was just one of those days that you hope passes real soon. I couldn't wait to go back home that morning.

At some point, during prep, I ran out of cigarettes. This was catastrophic. I asked the spot *dada*[23] to help me out. And he took me to Shrey sir.

I looked at him from a distance—he was wearing a white jacket.

What struck me about him was his smile. Oh, he smiled like a dream. I was feeling things I hadn't felt in months. Wait, years maybe. Forget butterflies, there were elephants doing salsa in my stomach. (It happens after a bad relationship, I am told. The first glimmer of genuine feeling comes with the full force of panic. Your body doesn't know better. It starts to feel like panic is the natural response to butterflies.)

We walked up to Shrey and asked how to get cigarettes. He passed on his cigarette. No major sentences were exchanged at this point between us,

---

[23] Elder brother.

but we were smoking together. It was weird. Good, but weird.

He was normal. And for women, that's a prerequisite to being around any man. She should feel safe. 'It's a vibe,' the women around you will tell you. Having lived most of our lives dodging the bad touch of men who casually walk around wanting to harass us, one develops a sort of filter to read vibes. Shrey was all good vibes from the word go!

He smoked with me and walked off after a few minutes. But before he left, he said, 'Even if the shoot wraps at 2 a.m., leave only after sunrise. The area isn't safe.' In hindsight, I appreciate even more the sort of guy he is. He is mindful of safety and takes care of people's comfort. That's just who he is.

That day, it didn't register. I had gone all guns blazing to my producer and asked how he could have miscalculated the plan. I had to fly back to Lucknow the next day and it was impossible to pack in a full night's sleep and catch the flight for 3 p.m. the next day.

The producer was zapped; he tried to wing it saying, 'No, it's not that bad.' He took me to Shrey again and said, 'Shrey, how can you scare our actors by saying the area is not safe.' Shrey was eating something. He looked up, glared and said, '*Jo sach hai, woh sach hai. Tumhare actor ke liye jhooth thodi bolunga.*' (What is true is true. I won't lie for your actor.)

I was dumbfounded for a bit but mostly amused. My mind was blown. He had something that I had not seen in someone in a very long time. Spine. Remember Aman, and how completely devoid of backbone he was? You can imagine my surprise.

At that moment, he had me. Oh yeah, he had me at hello!

I spent the day watching Shrey on set. My eyes kept following him. There was fluttering in my heart every time I looked at Shrey. The mere sight of him seemed to ignite a spark within me, creating a magnetic pull that I couldn't resist.

In those stolen moments of observation, it was almost as if time stood still and the world around us blurred into the background. The fluttering in my heart persisted. Love at first sight may sound like a cliché, but in that moment, it became my reality.

You know you are crushing hard when you text your best friend. I did that. Ishita was neck-deep in work and I made her dump all of it to hear me out. And rightly so—she was way more excited than me.

'I feel like talking to a boy after a long time,' I said to her. She egged me on to go strike a conversation with Shrey.

Having girlfriends as cheerleaders is like having a squad that can flip between being your hype team

19 February 2021: Hitting my rock bottom in Goa.

Winning my first award ever for comedy.

January 2021: When Coco's magic came into our lives.

Even when I left Lucknow to move on, I couldn't leave Coco—my ultimate source of happiness.

1 January 2023, Dubai: I proposed to Shrey literally at the top of the world—Burj Khalifa.

Look at that smile. Also, it's the first time I ever sat on my knees for a guy.

Dream proposal at Nusa Penida, Bali, 6 a.m.:
'Perfect does exist.'

The moment where I truly felt, '*Jo hota hai*, best *ke liye
hota hai*' (Whatever happens, happens for the best).

Shaadi *ho gayi bhai*, *meri*, like for real.

Our first trip together ever in Goa. Goa knows my most vulnerable self.

Yuvraj Dua being the 'Rocky Randhawa' of my life (he was actually the dialect coach for Ranveer in the film)

Pooja and Vagmi: Two friends who helped me heal after I moved to another city to get over my breakup.

Vagmi, my flatmate, my lifemate, my saviour, my BFF. After Coco, she is my second healer.

The most iconic series, *Every Male Best Friend Ever*, was derived from my past. Sanyam (Sharma) played a vital role in it.

Diwali 2020: When I was going through the worst time of my life, the only people who made me happy were my family members.

and your mischief consultants. Need a confidence boost? They're on it, lifting you higher than the highest heels. But watch out, because sometimes their encouragement to 'just go for it' might involve pushing you into the chaos of a blunder.

The beauty of it all is whether you're soaring high or navigating an epic misfire, it's like having a fan club that's committed to being there for every victory dance and every graceful recovery from an epic stumble. In the grand circus of life, girlfriends are the ringleaders, ensuring that no matter what, the show goes on with laughter and love.

That day, her idea was for me to go and chat with him. 'What do I say? He is working,' I asked her, part irritated and part curious. I seriously wondered, what can I have a conversation with him about?

While I was looking at Shrey from the balcony, talking to people around him, I realized I wanted to be around him.

I was called in to shoot eventually. It was quick, simple and effortless. This guy was just so smooth at his work. No hiccups, conducted himself with grace, and was assertive and respectful. I might have grinned more than needed for the camera, but I didn't care. My heart had found some of its original colour again. It was beating again.

We wrapped up a little late in the night. As we had decided, I left after sunrise.

Before leaving, I went up to him and said, 'Thank you for a great shoot.' He was warm, gracious but very formal.

The Poo in me woke up again. *'Kaun hai ye, jisne dobara mud ke mujhe nahi dekha.* Who is he?' (The Poo in me woke up again. 'Who is this, who didn't turn around to look at me again?)

That day, I left for Lucknow to spend time with my family for a few days. Maybe it was the last time I would see him.

My friends would ask me if I sent him a friend request. I hadn't. Perhaps it was ego or the desi expectation that a boy would pursue me, but I had decided I would lie low. What's the point? It was a 'moo point', like Joey says.[24]

For days, I didn't follow him on the gram. Neither did he. Of course, it doesn't happen every day, but if he wasn't making any effort, I wouldn't either. It's not worth it.

And then one day, he followed me. And I followed him back almost within a second. But then, Shrey can win an award for playing it cool. He didn't message for a long time—almost a week.

---

[24] One of the leads from *Friends* (1994–2004) played by Matt LeBlanc.

My anxious heart kept thinking maybe he had someone in his life. I did something out of character. I called a mutual friend, who I had discovered on the gram when Shrey followed me, and asked him, 'I don't know your equation with the guy but I want to know about him.' I made it clear that he couldn't pass on the word that I had called. I trusted him not to.

My friend was surprised. 'Harshita Gupta is calling to enquire about a guy. Who is it?' he asked. It is honestly that rare for me to care about a guy. But Shrey struck me like a bolt. I didn't see it coming; I didn't expect it.

I asked him just one question—is Shrey single? If he was not, I would have dashed to the other end of the world.

Thankfully, he was. He was.

The very next day, Shrey commented on a story I had posted. And from there on, I knew I had to stop playing hard to get. I was an adult. And I liked someone. There was a vibe to us—it was catchy, heady and more than anything, happy. I didn't want to play games. I wanted to be myself and see where this goes.

Shrey was texting me but sparsely. He would take hours to reply. I was beginning to feel he wasn't interested. But then one day, he asked me when I was to be back in Delhi. I was back that weekend. We made a plan to meet.

There are some telling signs when someone who enters your life is meant to stay. I knew that about Shrey when I was in the car going for our first date. All the other boys I had loved before disappeared from my mind. It was a clean slate.

He was fifteen minutes late. I wasn't sure whether to side-hug him or hold his hand. I was awkward. But Shrey being Shrey just sat down without any of the usual pleasantries. He was too focused on ordering food. He told me tricks on how to hold my drink. We chatted and laughed a lot.

But what is the difference between the boy you date and the boy you would want to marry eventually? Effort. After we left, he came to my house in Noida to drop me. He lives in North Delhi and Noida could well be called another planet. But it didn't matter to him. He insisted on dropping me.

I invited him upstairs. He had heard about my room throughout our date, and wanted to check it out too. He settled in comfortably and we started playing chess. He was bloody good, and I lost to him. My heart too . . .

When Ishita returned home, she hugged him with the sort of joy that only I could relate to. She was happy for me. But Shrey wasn't as expressive as us. He felt really weird. But he didn't let it show. He warmly stayed on and chatted with her about her life. What I admire about him is how he is such an attentive person. He is all-in when he is talking to someone. He remembered the details. I guess I had come to realize that he cared. And that was his love language.

When it was time for him to leave, I was strangely sad. I didn't want to let him go. But I had to, for time to take its course. It was then, the first time since we met, he opened his arms to give a hug. In that embrace, I felt the safest I ever had. I felt like a baby, being comforted.

He did not kiss me. He smiled. We both knew what had happened. He looked into my eyes, and said, 'I will see you again.'

He came home every week after that. But he wouldn't kiss me. I was wondering if he didn't find me attractive. I think in a world where special things are so easily accessible, we forget romance. Shrey wasn't like that. He knew this mattered to him. He knew he cared. He knew love was special. And he savoured the good things.

It happened most perfectly. He had come over for a round of chess. We had been seeing each other for a month. We had settled into a ritual—he would come over, we would chill, play chess and record the scores in our little black book. That evening, I won. I was leading by two extra wins in my kitty. He sheepishly noted the scores while I did a victory dance and then he passed the diary. It read: Can I kiss you?

My heart somersaulted. Yes, a thousand times over, please. He held me in his arms and kissed me.

I knew there was nowhere else in the world I would
rather be.

The first time I realized it had happened,
Was that evening we first met.
Tripping, falling, barely walking, amidst a lot of
laughing,
I felt your strong hands holding me, every time
I slipped.
A few steps down the line,
I knew you were there to catch me
If I fall . . .
Reassurances are a funny thing.
They show up right when you stop
needing them.

I saw you through the rays of the setting sun . . .
Your smile brighter than that golden gleam on
the horizon

Did I hear my heart skip a beat?
Nah, not possible.

Your mind can be a funny thing. It never stops
playing games . . .

That evening over that glass of fizzy brews,
We laid bare our hearts.
The pain of broken pasts and a thousand
unfulfilled dreams.

At one point, I looked up and for the first time
in a while . . .
I felt someone had heard me beyond my words
I covered it up quickly with a wisecrack . . .
Sealed it with a joke; lest you get a peek into
matters of my messy heart.
Faith is a funny thing. Once shaken and broken,
it continues to find reasons to disbelieve

It was a long ride home that night after our
first date.
Our fingers intertwined, our thoughts
entangled . . .
For the first time in a while, it didn't feel alone.
You chatted about my favourite things
Like I mattered.
When have I ever mattered?
I stared at you mesmerized . . .

Something tugged at me when you left . . .

I felt my hand not letting yours go . . .
Let go, I chided myself.

I really didn't want to though
Now that's the thing about hope . . .
It's funny really.
Just when you give up on the universe,
Something unexpected takes your breath away.

FROM AC'S DESK

German Psychoanalyst Eric Fromm sums up the idea of love in a succinct way in his book *The Art of Loving.* He says, 'Love is a decision, it is a judgement, it is a promise. If love were only a feeling, there would be no basis for the promise to love each other forever. A feeling comes and it may go. How can I judge that it will stay forever, when my act does not involve judgement and decision.'[25]

As we progress through one of my favourite books, it reads, 'Love isn't something natural. Rather it requires discipline, concentration, patience, faith, and the overcoming of narcissism. It isn't a feeling; it is a practice.'

In a way, he says that love isn't a transitory feeling, but a commitment we make to ourselves to love the other. We tend to confuse romance, lust and being drawn to the person in the initial phases as love. That is largely just that—attraction. Love often begins when the initial rush has subsided into a more mundane every day and two people have learnt to love each other for their personhood and true self. You might smirk and say, too idealistic! While I will not argue that, ask anyone who has chosen to be with the one they loved and committed too, it's going beyond the here and now,

---

[25] Eric Fromm, *The Art of Loving* (UK: Thorsons, 2010).

toiling through the differences, continuous repair-rupture, growing and evolving together. Intention towards the union has been the most important secret sauce of the longevity.

As I write this, English poet Elizabeth Barrett Browning's sonnet 'How Do I Love Thee' comes to mind.[26]

I love thee with a love I seemed to lose
With my lost saints. I love thee with the breath,
Smiles, tears, of all my life; and, if God choose,
I shall but love thee better after death.

In modern love, however, this looks like a far truth. There seems to be an emerging pattern of not moving beyond the initial attraction—attachment dance. If you take a quick glance at user generated content sites like Quora, you will find people blaming social media, hiding behind screens, dating site breadcrumbing-ghosting patterns, individualism, lack of effort and plethora of other options as some of the reasons as to why long-term stable relationships are becoming a challenge for young people.

So, what is the cure, you may be tempted to ask. In return, may I suggest care instead of cure.

---

[26] Elizabeth Barrett Browning, 'How Do I Love Thee? (Sonnet 43)', Poets.org, https://poets.org/poem/how-do-i-love-thee-sonnet-43.

Care, caring enough, caring enough for oneself to delve into the discovery of who we truly are, what our true intentions in the relationship are, what is our motivation, why do we want a relationship, what are we seeking in it and who is truly compatible as opposed to who is available. Would you care to sit with these questions for a while and not rush into finding a proverbial cure?

6

What Happens After Happily Ever After?

Have you noticed that all fairy tales conclude with relationships characterized by the joyful certainty of 'and then they all lived happily ever after'. In our childhood fantasies, we might have envisioned ourselves as protagonists in our own fairy tales, patiently awaiting our true love. Once found, we believed life would transform into a magical, effortless existence, filled with songs and dancing birds. It's almost as if love would ensure a perpetually idyllic existence. Or so we thought.

WRONG.

The day after you realize you are in love with someone is often followed by anxiety of paramount proportions; anxiety you can barely make sense of; anxiety that feels alien. Happy, dramatic, stunning and fairy tale-like relationships that often entertain thoughts like, 'If only I had more money, a child, a different job. If only I looked different or lived in

113

a nicer neighbourhood. Then maybe, just maybe, I could live 'happily ever after.'

However, the reality is that healthy, strong relationships aren't built on careers, social status, appearance or wealth. Successful and satisfying long-term relationships demand serious effort. Partners must master effective communication, dedicate time and space for each other and learn to appreciate moments without distractions from phones and devices.

The pervasive notion that there will be a time when our relationship is effortlessly and consistently happy is a recurring theme not just in movies and books but also in popular narrative. Why else do we say Shah Rukh Khan and Gauri Khan are the 'it couple' with their dreamy seaside home and three perfect children. We gaze at images of celebrities, strolling with their children, eagerly consume gossip about their lives and speculate on the state of their love and personal affairs. We even join names for iconic couples like 'Brangelina' or 'Saifeena' back home.

But wait, let's deconstruct what happens after happily-ever-after shall we?

1. The reality check: life continues

Life is a relentless journey, unfolding beyond the milestones. The problems occur when we have a checklist waiting to tick something off. I always wanted to be married and after Aman, I was looking for a partner who would fit my bill.

On my first few dates with Shrey, I wanted to cartwheel around Delhi, singing like Preity Zinta from *Kal Ho Na Ho*, in a red dress, with a bunch of red flowers.

I was drunk on love.

However, the reality is far more dynamic, akin to a river that ceaselessly meanders through uncharted terrain.

Consider the accomplished professional who secures their dream job after years of dedicated effort. In the jubilation of this career triumph, it may seem as though life has reached a pinnacle. Yet, as the days unfold, new challenges emerge. Perhaps the complexities of leadership, navigating office dynamics or adapting to evolving industry trends. The achievement of one goal unveils a fresh set of opportunities and hurdles.

Relationships, too, are not exempt from this perpetual motion. The commitment made is not an end but only a commencement. It signifies the initiation of a journey where the partners intertwine their destinies, bound not by a finite destination but by the continuous exploration of each other and experiences.

Consider the couple who, after overcoming the hurdles of courtship, stands hand in hand on the threshold of marriage. It is not the end of their story but the start of a shared narrative—one that will be written through moments of joy, growth and discovery.

I remember attending the wedding anniversary of a couple I know. Let's call her X and him Y. They celebrated their twenty-fifth wedding anniversary with great joy. As they reminisced about their journey, over champagne, it became evident that the key to their enduring love was not the day they said 'I do', but the countless 'I choose you' moments that followed. In one of the toasts, they recounted their worst fight. 'It was almost the end I thought,' said X. And then Y took over and said, 'I stayed up all night, writing the most elaborate resignation letter of my life, and somehow, as the words flowed, I realized I was drafting an apology. I didn't want to let this go ever. I wanted this, every day till the end. Fidelity, marriage, commitment, it's all a choice you make.' As he kissed her, I remember thinking that life threw challenges their way—career changes, raising children and personal transformations—but each hurdle became a stepping stone, propelling them forward in their shared love for each other.

On the drive back home, I thought of them and told myself the most important bit about relationships—they are an ever-evolving love affair, where sometimes, you aren't even fully in love, but you still stay. Partners navigate the intricate steps of understanding, compromise and mutual support.

The honeymoon phase may fade, but in its wake emerges a more profound connection forged through weathered storms.

Relationships are like partnerships. You are equals in it together, so you might as well operate like a well-oiled unit.

Over the years, Shrey and my love evolved from the innocent excitement of firsts to the mature and steadfast bond of adulthood. We didn't even have a honeymoon period, per se. But we were honest and ourselves from the word go.

The challenges we faced—long-distance, career changes and personal growth—only made us stronger. Unlike the movies, life did not pause after that night when we kissed for the first time.

2. Flawless is a myth

In a world inundated with images of perfection, both in the glossy pages of magazines and the curated feeds of social media, the concept of flawlessness has become a coveted but elusive ideal. Flawless is a myth—an unattainable standard that sets us up for perpetual dissatisfaction and self-doubt.

3. I am not flawless. Neither is Shrey. And that is okay.

When it comes to physical appearance, society often dictates an unattainable standard of flawless skin. The beauty industry capitalizes on this notion, bombarding consumers with products promising blemish-free, radiant skin. However, the reality is that flawless skin is not a reality. I remember bumping into a well-known actress at my dermatologist's clinic. I was having a particularly bad day. My zits weren't making me feel very perky either. And then, I saw her. She was drop-dead gorgeous on screen. But here she was standing without a shred of makeup on her face, completely bare-skinned—her pores and blemishes were showing. So real, so beautiful. It's like that famous scene in Barbie when Barbie meets a real woman. 'You are beautiful,' she tells the old lady—her skin wrinkly, pigmentation visible. She replies, 'I know.'

Every individual bears the marks of their journey. Be it acne scars, freckles or the passage of time etched in fine lines. These so-called imperfections are not flaws; rather, they are the chapters of a person's life story, each mark telling a tale of resilience, growth and experience.

Similarly, in romance, the myth of flawlessness manifests in the unrealistic expectations perpetuated by fairy tales and romantic comedies. These narratives often portray relationships as seamless, with perfect couples navigating life without a single disagreement. However, the truth is that no relationship is flawless. Love is complex.

Embracing the imperfections of a partner and the relationship itself is not a sign of weakness, but a show of your commitment to love.

People are expert hide-and-seek champions when it comes to their struggles. It's like they've enrolled in a top-secret mission to conceal the messy fights, secret rendezvous and solo dance parties of loneliness. Disney, with its fairy-tale magic, conveniently forgets to showcase the real drama—the dirty socks on the floor or the toilet seat that mysteriously turns into a splash zone. They conveniently skip the soundtrack of doors slamming. It's a world where reality is hidden and the messy, smelly bits are left off-camera.

But life isn't like that. Nothing real can begin unless you lose the facade. Talk about your farts or burps, share embarrassing life incidents, discuss the taste of boogers, and whether you've peed in a swimming pool. Be yourself.

It took me a few weeks to do this. Initially, I would be all ready to welcome him at the door. Hair done, lipstick in place, even if it was just an evening at home. It took some time to believe that without that expensive blush, that compact and the foundation, he still loved me.

We dated for weeks, but it only became a relationship when I stopped trying to impress him and just started being myself—quite unhinged, rather messy, very short tempered, sometimes a bit bitchy and totally in love with him.

The bad comes with the good and vice versa.

4. Honeymoon every day of your life, not just a few months

No, I am not suggesting you be in a permanent state of leisure or make a long vacation of your existence. But hear me out. Honeymooning should be a long-term thing. If it lasts only for six months, it's balderdash. In romantic relationships, the honeymoon phase has long been hailed as the golden period—a time when love is in full bloom, and everything seems to sparkle with the ethereal glow of perfection. However, as we journey through the intricacies of human connection, it becomes increasingly evident that this phase is more of a blur than a lasting reality. Instead of chasing this fleeting illusion, couples should actively cast it aside and embrace authenticity from day one, laying the foundation for a more meaningful and sustainable connection.

The honeymoon phase is often characterized by intense passion, overwhelming infatuation and a seemingly endless stream of romantic gestures. Couples find themselves enraptured in the novelty of their union, revelling in the joy of discovering each other's quirks and virtues. Yet, behind the enchanting facade, lies a crucial truth—it is not sustainable in the long run. You can't play the larger-than-life Shah Rukh Khan every day of your life. So, might as well be you, no?

As the initial fervour of a relationship subsides, many couples may feel disheartened, questioning the authenticity of their connection. The truth is that the honeymoon phase is not indicative of a relationship's depth or potential for longevity. It is merely a starting point, a prelude to the real work that lies ahead. By acknowledging this, couples can release the pressure of living up to an unrealistic ideal and instead focus on building a foundation rooted in genuine connection.

This honeymoon phase often leads couples to present idealized versions of themselves, creating a false sense of compatibility. When people allow themselves to be vulnerable, flaws and all, they invite their partner to do the same. This openness fosters a deeper understanding, laying the groundwork for a relationship based on genuine connection rather than superficial illusions.

Being authentic from day one requires a willingness to communicate honestly. It involves sharing not only the joys but also the challenges, fears and insecurities that make us human. This level of transparency builds trust and resilience within the relationship as couples navigate the complexities of life together, hand in hand.

Moreover, authenticity empowers individuals to maintain a strong sense of self within the partnership.

Rather than conforming to societal or relationship expectations, each person can express their true self, fostering a dynamic where both partners can grow and evolve together.

5. Grow individually to grow together

While love is often portrayed as a profound connection between two souls, it is equally a catalyst for individual metamorphosis—a journey of self-discovery and personal evolution.

Your love should help both partners embark on a transformative expedition, challenging each other to rise above their limitations and blossom into the best versions of themselves. Love becomes a nurturing ground, not only for the relationship to thrive but also for the individuals within it to flourish. It is a constant interplay between supporting your partner and growing together.

Championing your partner is more than just standing by them in moments of triumph or offering a comforting embrace in times of defeat. It also involves actively participating in each other's personal growth, encouraging the pursuit of dreams and fostering an environment where both partners can unfurl their wings and soar. It's about becoming each other's biggest cheerleaders.

Yet, love is not a one-way street. It demands a reciprocal commitment to self-improvement, an acknowledgement that personal growth is not only an individual endeavour but also a gift to the relationship. As individuals evolve, the partnership itself undergoes a shift, adapting to the changing needs, aspirations and nuances of each.

One of my biggest learnings was the willingness to communicate openly, share fears and aspirations and provide unwavering support even when faced with the uncertainties that come with change. Love, in its truest form, is actually a safe space.

6. They will annoy you—live with it

Relationships are crafted to test our patience. A person who knows you that well will figure out your triggers and buttons. It's simpler to navigate life solo, free from scrutiny or the need to acknowledge what's wrong with us. However, the essence of being in a relationship lies in confronting discomfort and cultivating awareness. The expectation that love should effortlessly flow is a misconception. Often, it indicates avoidance of more challenging issues. Embracing mistakes is key to being in a healthy equation. Drop the ego, when you fuck up, learn to apologize.

Numerous challenges in relationships stem from seemingly mundane aspects of daily life. For instance, differing rituals in households is a major hurdle in India. 'That's not how we do it at my home'. Find the middle ground to this difference as soon as possible.

Smaller issues may include different energy levels, disapproval of a partner's friend, holiday plans etc.

More significant obstacles such as financial burdens, temperamental issues or divergent views on life choices can also emerge.

When faced with disagreements, doubts about the strength of the bond may surface. At this juncture, three paths present themselves. First, one may choose to exit the relationship, realizing that the person doesn't align with their priorities. Second, confronting and resolving the issue together can become a transformative experience, reinforcing the positive aspects of the relationship. Lastly, maintaining the status quo without addressing underlying issues can hinder personal and relationship growth, a choice advised against.

This phase is pivotal in defining the essence of love. It prompts people to acknowledge whether certain aspects are deal-breakers or if they are willing to undergo the necessary growth to address challenges. Know your deal breakers and just make peace with the fact that they will annoy you.

I repeat, love is a choice you make.

7. Learn to trust

I know very few people who haven't been cheated on—both men and women. And once bitten, always shy. Even when things go hunky-dory and brilliantly, you'll look at your partner and think, 'Is he too good to be true? What's wrong with him?' This happened to me for a very long time. I would have this nagging need to break into Shrey's phone and check his messages. He gave me no reason to be suspicious. But it became second nature for me with Aman, and once I fell in love again, the patterns persisted.

I thought of all the worst-case scenarios and was cranky, jumpy, and marinating in my overthinking.

Assessing the breadth and depth of trust within a relationship becomes a crucial step in understanding and defining love.

Contrary to the perception of trust as a binary concept, it gradually evolves through consistent actions, thoughts and words. Trust based solely on kindness is cautioned against; rather, trust should be built through the gradual sharing of oneself and observing the reciprocation of honesty. Each preceding phase in the relationship contributes to the foundation of trust.

Trust starts with self-trust, requiring alignment between thoughts, words and actions. You must consistently follow through on communicated needs or desires, individuals establish a sense of trustworthiness. This mutual demonstration of reliability shows reciprocal trust and understanding.

Trust in others is fostered when they create a sense of safety, make healthy decisions and align their lives with shared values. One of the things I really appreciated about Shrey is his patience. He valued me. He understood me from a deeper space. He always

asked, where was this coming from, and he never lost
his cool on me.

Evaluating trust involves considering three
spaces: physical trust, mental trust and emotional
trust. Physical trust is cultivated when one feels safe
and cared for in the presence of their partner. Mental
trust pertains to trusting their thought processes and
decision-making abilities. Emotional trust involves
trusting their values, behaviour and treatment
of others.

It's acknowledged that absolute trust across all
dimensions may not be immediate and individuals
are prone to making mistakes that may challenge
trust. Open communication is vital to maintaining
trust as dishonesty, secrets or gaslighting can erode it.

As a practical exercise, recognizing and
appreciating daily acts of trust becomes a powerful
tool. Expressing gratitude for consistent efforts, even
in routine actions, reinforces trust and reliability.
Say thank you every time. Don't take goodness
for granted.

8. Fights are healthy—*daag acche hai*[27]

Sorry to dunk you in some Surf Excel messaging. But
I stand by this. I will tell you two reasons why.

---

[27] Stains are nice.

I know a couple. They met on an app and had the best date of their lives. On their first date, they chatted for twelve hours. Next one, just as many hours. They moved fast. They were in love within a month. They were perfect. And they never fought. Guess what happened to them? Six months later, he broke up with her one fine morning. He didn't give any solid reasons and just said—I don't feel the way you feel.

Look closely now, there were grouses. These two only focused on the good bits. They were scared to look at the negative aspects of their relationship. I suspect there were unsaid things that festered and caused the end of them.

Constructive conflict, when approached skilfully, proves beneficial for relationships. The vitality of long-term relationships doesn't hinge on dazzling date nights or memorable holidays. They don't solely endure due to the presence of good friends, although community support certainly contributes to relationship stability. Instead, a pivotal factor in the longevity of a relationship lies in the art of handling disagreements.

When partners adeptly express anger to each other in healthy ways, they cultivate essential qualities and abilities. These qualities, including compassion, empathy and patience, serve as the foundation for understanding challenges.

This brings me to my most important learning.

It's an incident I am not proud of. It's an incident that is too deeply a personal failing that I never want to revisit. But I want to write about it, so you all know that such things can happen and that it needs to be worked on.

Shrey and I had a terrible fight once. It started over something small then became bigger then even bigger and then the decibels rose, and I shouted at him. His mother was around, and she heard our voices. Visibly scared, almost mortified, she stared at us shell shocked. We both knew that the fight had to be paused.

The next day we spoke and made two rules:

1. Never go to bed angry.
2. Never shout at each other in front of anyone. Follow the closed-door policy and never disrespect each other in public.

It's been years, but we have stood by this every time during every fight. Our relationship shouldn't scare our families or scar us for lives. Let's be kind even in our worst moments.

9. *Kya karoge itna* ego *leke*? (What will you do with this much ego?)

The instinct to enter an argument to prove oneself right is entirely natural. The notion of being right provides validation and a convenient outlet for placing blame on others. It establishes a sense of security in our beliefs and assumptions, allowing us to avoid any need for personal change or responsibility. While the concept of winning and being right may prevail in competitive environments, such as competitions, politics, or war, it proves ineffective in the realm of relationships. In this context, being right doesn't resolve the underlying issue. Although our ego might enjoy a momentary boost, the problem is likely to resurface, and the relationship remains unaffected by the so-called resolution. In essence, ego-driven victories result in a loss for both parties.

Contrary to the pursuit of being right, our primary objective should be understanding. The ultimate aim is connection and growth, not merely conflict resolution. In the dynamics of a relationship, if one partner wins and the other loses, it's a mutual loss. The only triumph in an argument is one in which both parties emerge victorious. Recognizing and internalizing this principle is vital for the health of the relationship.

Acknowledging that 'I'm right, and you're right' or 'you're wrong, and so am I' leads to win-win scenarios. Temporarily setting aside our egos to confront and overcome challenges with our partners serves to purify the ego. This purification involves relinquishing the desire to be the centre of attention, paving the way for increased understanding, empathy, compassion, trust and love for both individuals.

As a practical exercise, try identifying your ego and passion amid a conflict. Recognizing these elements allows for a conscious effort to set them aside, facilitating a more constructive and harmonious resolution with your partner.

Identify the fundamental issue. Even though our commitment is to engage in constructive arguments, not every disagreement begins on that positive note. There are instances when emotions boil over, leading to explosive situations. In these moments, rather than prolonging the argument or dismissing it altogether, take the time to diagnose what went wrong. This reflective approach also diminishes the likelihood of encountering the same conflict in the future. With practice in navigating productive arguments, one may develop the ability to shift into this mode instantly. However, if that isn't the case, both individuals can choose to step away from the argument temporarily, reflect on their contributions to the matter, and then come back prepared to share those insights with their partner.

Our anger is often misdirected, leading us to argue about seemingly trivial issues when the underlying source of frustration lies elsewhere. For instance, a disagreement about household chores might be a smokescreen for dissatisfaction with how our partner allocates their time. Similarly, debates about routines might be a manifestation of a deeper need for attention from our partners. When conflicts centre on household responsibilities, the root cause may be a feeling of being misunderstood or unheard. Resolving the conflict becomes elusive until we accurately identify and address its true origin. Attempting to correct a specific behaviour, like ensuring a partner refrains from smiling at others, may offer temporary relief. However, lasting resolution requires delving into the genuine issue, such as addressing insecurities, to truly resolve the conflict.

Like diversity in love languages, individuals also possess distinct approaches to handling conflicts. Recognizing how each person processes disagreement facilitates a better understanding of arguments and promotes a more impartial perspective. While I prefer immediate discussion to address issues, Shrey leans towards taking a break to collect his thoughts and cool down before engaging in conversation. My inclination is towards a swift resolution, whereas he values the opportunity to decompress and ponder the matter independently before coming back together. Embracing this awareness about each other prevented me from feeling hurt when he opted for silence during an argument, and it spared him from irritation when I desired a more extended discussion. Identifying your partner's fight style, as well as recognizing your own, represents the initial stride in advocating for love during conflicts.

10. Say I love you and mean every word

I have a theory about dishonesty. If you say things you don't mean, then you are just a liar. I took a long time to say I love you. I wanted to really mean it when I said it.

Expressing love comes with varying interpretations and expectations. Saying I love you is often a pivotal moment. Some perceive it as a commitment for a lifelong partnership, while for others, it might signify a desire for a more immediate connection. The spectrum of intentions between these extremes is vast and some may say it as a reflex, driven solely by the emotion of the moment. And others want to really mean it, when it is said.

Just in the interest of ending this chapter on a moment of hope, I will tell you my story of the first I love you I ever said to Shrey.

It was six months into our dating life. It was all going well. I was on cloud nine every time I was around him. I would often just look at him and wonder—'Did I really luck out?' Like that Fawad Khan line in *Humsafar* (2011): *'Tum mujhe kisi naeki ke badle mili ho'* (I got you in return for some good deed). But the words were never said. Like they were never needed. He knew and I knew. Right?

Yes, it was my heart. It was scared to find its strength again. If people who have known you for decades can shatter you, is it worth loving again? It was almost as if, if I said the words, it would all become too real. If it got too real, something bad would happen to it. I didn't want to jinx it. To be able to believe that it was really happening for me, was unimaginable. Let's just say I was scared that if I got too happy or too comfortable, it would all get taken away from me. No one gets everything in life and Shrey was the one thing I didn't want to lose ever. He was that perfect, he was that precious.

But one day, my heart was so full of love that the words just had to come out of my mouth. It was inevitable. One night after a great dinner, I was drinking some wine. I was cuddling up with him and sometime after the second bottle, I said it to him: 'I love you.' He smiled, and said, 'I love you too'. He realized I was drunk and half-passed out, so he put the duvet on me before putting me to sleep.

Every time since then, I have meant my words. Especially and mostly, I love you. For the first time, it was sponsored by my heart and Yellowtail Rose. Liquid courage for the first one and honesty for the rest of my life.

FROM AC'S DESK

When it comes to love, great artists and writers have travelled to places before psychologists have. I, for one, borrow my words from them sometimes. A bit of poetry is known to soothe broken hearts always. So, whether you prefer plugging in a ghazal, an Adele number, a Taylor Swift song or a heavy metal track, I am sending your way a poem by poet and playwright Derek Alton Walcott:[28]

You will love again the stranger who was your self.
Give wine. Give bread, Give back your heart
to itself, to the stranger who has loved you
all your life, whom you ignored
for another, who knows you by heart.

---

[28] Derek Alton Walcott, 'Love After Love', Allpoetry.com, https://allpoetry.com/love-after-love.

7

Simplifying Modern-Day Dating Lingo for Romantics

Once upon a time, relationships followed a script as straightforward as a '90s sitcom plotline. Two people met, sparks flew, they fell madly in love and the credits rolled. Cue applause. Fast forward to the present, and the dating world is more of a 'Choose your own adventure' novel, written in invisible ink on a rollercoaster.

Welcome to this chapter where we toss aside the rose-coloured glasses and take a daring plunge into the swirling whirlpool of modern romance. Relationships these days are less of 'happily ever after' and more of 'let's see how this goes . . . and maybe consult a survival guide'.

In the era of swipes, likes and emojis that convey emotions even Shakespeare couldn't have imagined, decoding relationships feels like trying to solve a

Sudoku puzzle designed by a naughty wizard. It has more twists and turns than a soap opera script on caffeine.

In the labyrinth of contemporary courtship, be prepared for plot twists, unexpected cliffhangers and characters who ghost faster than a phantom in a haunted mansion. Buckle up, because in the dating maze, the only thing guaranteed is that nothing is guaranteed.

Let's dive into the chaos, decode the signals and emerge on the other side with our sanity and sense of humour intact. It's time to rewrite the rules and find comedy in the chaos of twenty-first-century love.

Scenario 1

A: 'I don't know what's wrong with me. I just can't . . . fall in love.'

B: (pauses, considering) 'Hey, maybe you're aromantic.'

A furrows their brow. 'Aromantic? Is that like not being into flowers or something?'

B chuckles softly. 'Not quite. It's more about not feeling romantic attraction to others. You know, like how some people just aren't into superhero movies or jazz music? It's just a different way of experiencing relationships.'

A nods slowly, beginning to understand. 'So, it's not about being broken or missing out on something?'

B shakes their head. 'Exactly! Being aromantic is just one of many ways people experience love and relationships. It's not better or worse, just different.'

A smiles, feeling a weight lift off their shoulders. 'Well, that's a relief. I guess I've just been looking for something that's not in my nature.'

B grins. 'Exactly! You're just being true to yourself. And who needs grand romantic gestures anyway? I bet you'll find your own unique way to connect with people.'

A laughs, feeling a newfound sense of freedom. 'You know what? You're right. Maybe I'll embrace my inner secret agent and navigate the world of relationships on my own terms.'

B raises an eyebrow playfully. 'And who knows? Maybe instead of a decoder ring, you'll get a cool gadget that lets you see the world in a whole new way.'

A grins, feeling excited about the possibilities ahead. 'Now that's a mission I can get behind.'

Definition of aromantic: Aromanticism is a romantic orientation characterized by a lack of romantic interest or a limited desire for romantic relationships. People who identify as aromantic may still experience other forms of attraction, such as platonic or aesthetic attraction, but they do not typically experience the same level of romantic attraction as those who identify as romantic.

Harshita speaks: *Kyunki inko aata hi nahi hai, inko pata hi nahi, inse hota hi nahi hai. Hopeless romantic ki zindagi barbaad ho gayi.* (Because they don't know, they don't understand, and they can't do anything. The life of a hopeless romantic has been ruined.)

Scenario 2

A: 'She only ever seems to text me after I've given up on hearing from her.'

B: 'Ah, the classic "I'll-subtly-reappear-when-you've-moved-on" tactic.' That's textbook benching, my friend.'

A sighed, feeling like they were caught in a dating drama series with too many plot twists. 'Benching? Seriously? I didn't even know we were playing a sport. What's next? Penalty kicks for missed date opportunities?'

B chuckled, leaning back as if sharing the wisdom of the dating oracle. 'Dating is the Olympics of emotions, my dear friend. Bench-warming is just one of the many events.'

A raised an eyebrow. 'So, what's my strategy here? Do I start doing push-ups and jumping jacks to stay in the game?'

B smirked. 'Nah, that's too old school. The next time she texts, hit her with a hurdle. Something like, "Oh, sorry, I was too busy mastering the art of patience."'

A: Mastering patience?'

B winked. 'Exactly. Show her you're not just a player. And if she tries to bench you again, well, let her know you're too busy.'

Definition of benching: It refers to a dating behaviour where one person keeps another person interested but at a distance, without committing to a serious relationship. The person who is 'benching' may engage in occasional communication or dates but will avoid becoming fully involved. It's a term used to describe a situation where someone is being kept on the 'bench' as a backup option without a commitment.

> Harshita speaks: *Na pyaar karenge, na kisi aur ko karne denge.* Stop being a *delulu* and the *solulu* is just to accept that they don't love you. (Neither will they love you, nor will they let anyone else love you. Stop being delusional; the solution is simply to accept that they don't love you.)

Scenario 3

A: 'She replies to every second or third message I send her but never wants to meet IRL.'

B: Raising an eyebrow knowingly. 'Ah, the breadcrumbing conundrum. Classic move.'

A sighed. 'Breadcrumbing? Is that the modern version of leaving a trail of crumbs to find your way out of a confusing relationship?'

B chuckled, leaning in as if sharing the secrets of the dating detective's handbook. 'Close, but it's more like leaving just enough crumbs to keep you following, but never leading you to the treasure chest of an actual date.'

A frowned. 'So, I'm stuck with no prize at the end?'

B nodded sympathetically. 'The key is to lay low for a while. Let her see what life is like without your delightful messages. If she's genuinely interested, she'll start dropping more than breadcrumbs. If not, well, at least you've saved yourself from a headache.'

Definition of breadcrumbing: In the context of dating and relationships, breadcrumbing refers to manipulative and misleading behaviour where one person gives another person intermittent and small signals of romantic or emotional interest without any genuine intention of pursuing a committed relationship. The term is derived from the idea that the person is leaving breadcrumbs—tiny morsels of attention or affection—to keep the other person interested without making a significant investment.

Harshita speaks: Hello, you little piece of toy. You are just in their life so they don't get bored. What a killjoy!

Scenario 4

A: 'She always has a different excuse not to meet me.'

B: Leans in with a sceptical expression. 'Sounds like you're being catfished, my friend."

A squinted, imagining a scenario where fishing rods and virtual ponds collided in the world of online dating. 'Catfished? Does that involve actual fish or am I missing some new dating slang?'

B chuckled, shaking their head. 'No fish involved, but plenty of deceptive swimming. Catfishing is when someone lures you in with a virtual persona, but meeting in real life seems to be as elusive as a unicorn on roller skates.'

A sighed, feeling like they were in the midst of a dating detective drama. 'So, I'm just entangled in someone's web of excuses?'

B nodded, playing the part of the seasoned investigator. 'Exactly. If every meet-up plan dissolves faster than a sugar cube in hot tea, it's time to cast doubt.'

A raised an eyebrow. 'How do I expose this catfish if they're swimming in the murky waters of excuses?'

B smirked, as if revealing the secret weapon in their dating detective kit. 'Request a video call. A real-time conversation can't hide behind the smoke and mirrors of text messages. If she's legit, great! If not, well, you might have just uncovered a feline in disguise.'

Definition of catfishing: To be catfished refers to the act of being deceived by someone online who creates a false identity, typically on a social media platform, to establish a fraudulent relationship. The term gained popularity after the 2010 documentary and subsequent MTV reality series called *Catfish*, which explored such deceptive online relationships. In a catfishing scenario, the person behind the false identity often uses fake photos, information, and sometimes an entirely made-up persona to engage with others. This deception can be for various reasons, such as seeking attention, emotional manipulation, or, in some cases, financial scams.

Harshita speaks: *Dhokha*[29] but without love and sex. Video calls are a must for face verification if you happen to meet them online.

Scenario 5

A: 'What is cuffing season?'

B chuckled. 'Cuffing season is when the weather gets colder, and people start looking for a cozy companion to share scarves, hot beverages, and possibly body heat with.'

---

[29] Betrayal.

A sighed; he had unwittingly become the mascot for seasonal snuggling.

B nodded, a conspiratorial glint in their eye. 'It's like nature's way of saying, "Hey, it's getting chilly. Time to find someone to Netflix and chill with."'

A: 'So, if I want to participate in cuffing season, all I need is a latte and a willing partner?'

B 'Sip wisely, my friend, and may your cuffing season be cozy and caffeine-fueled!'

Definition of cuffing season: Cuffing season is a colloquial term that refers to the time of year, typically during the fall and winter months, when people are more inclined to seek out and form romantic relationships. The idea behind cuffing season is that as the weather gets colder and the days become shorter, individuals may feel a desire for companionship and intimacy, leading them to pursue relationships.

Harshita speaks: Why try something that comes with an expiry date? The warmth of soup on a winter night is better than the warmth of the red flag you are trying to wrap yourself in.

Scenario 6

A: 'I do like her, but I'm still texting the other one just in case. Yeah, I guess I'm cushioning.'

B: Raising an eyebrow knowingly.. 'Keeping your options open like a dating acrobat.'

A looked sheepish, as if confessing to a clandestine act. 'It is like having a backup plan for my love life. Like a romantic safety net.'

B: 'Cushioning is like having a soft landing in case your main romantic endeavour takes an unexpected nosedive. So, you are not just talking to the second one, you are cushioning the emotional freefall?'

A: 'Bingo. Just in case.'

B smirked and said, 'As long as you're aware of the cushioning, play your cards wisely. Don't get smacked.'

Definition of cushioning: Cushioning, in the context of dating and relationships, refers to a behaviour where someone in a committed relationship keeps in contact with other potential romantic partners as a form of insurance or backup. Essentially, a person who is cushioning is maintaining connections with other individuals in case their current relationship doesn't work out.

Harshita speaks: Cheating that can be justified as best friends, best colleagues or best pal isn't the best for your existing relationship.

Scenario 7

A: 'At first, I thought I was asexual, but then I realized I can have sexual desire for people . . . just not until I really know them!'

B nodded understandingly. 'Sounds like you might be demisexual.'

A looked intrigued. 'Demisexual? Is that like a rare Pokemon or something?'

B chuckled, shaking their head. 'Not quite. Demisexuality is more like having a special filter on your romantic camera. You only develop feelings of attraction once a deep emotional connection has been established.'

A raised an eyebrow. 'So, it's like I have a 'get-to-know-you-well' switch for my romantic feelings?'

B nodded, playing the role of the demisexual spirit guide. 'Exactly. It's not about being uninterested in romance; it's about requiring a strong emotional foundation before the romantic spark ignites.'

A grinned, realizing they had stumbled upon the secret society of demisexuals. 'So, I'm not asexual; I'm just picky with my emotional investments. Like a love connoisseur.'

B chuckled. 'Precisely. Welcome to the demisexual club, where deep connections are the secret ingredient to unlocking the romantic vault. May your emotional bonds be strong, and your heart be discerning!'

Definition of demisexuality: Demisexuality is a sexual orientation characterized by a person experiencing sexual attraction only after developing a deep emotional or romantic connection with someone. Unlike individuals who may experience immediate sexual attraction based on physical appearance, demisexual individuals typically need a strong emotional bond or connection before feeling sexual desire.

Harshita speaks: Relationship where size matters but of emotions, connection and trust.

Scenario 8

A: 'She never responds to my messages, but texts me "u up" at 1 a.m.? What's the deal?'

B smirked knowingly. 'Sounds like you're getting firedoored, bud.'

A looked perplexed. 'Firedoored? Is that a new term for late-night locksmith services or something?'

B chuckled, shaking their head. 'No locksmiths involved, but it's about getting stuck in a one-way door of communication. She only contacts you when it suits her, leaving you metaphorically banging on the firedoor with no reply.'

A sighed, feeling like they had unwittingly become a character in a dating mystery novel. 'So, I'm not just receiving random "u up" texts; I'm in a one-sided communication maze?'

B nodded, the sage of unrequited messages. 'Exactly. The firedoor only swings one way, and it's not in your favour.'

A smirked, realizing they were caught in the crossfire of communication confusion. 'So, I'm not a priority; I'm just the backup plan for when the main door is closed. Lovely.'

B patted A on the back sympathetically.

Definition of firedoored: Firedoored refers to a situation where one person consistently tries to communicate or pursue a relationship with someone, but the other person consistently ignores or 'fires' them. In other words, it describes a one-sided and unreciprocated interaction where one person puts in effort, but the other person is not responsive or engaged.

> Harshita Speaks: *Ek tarfa pyaar*[30] is the worst feeling in the world, what a liar Karan Johar is.[31]

Scenario 9

A: 'I'm not feeling it any more, but she's really into me. I think I'm just going to ghost her.'

B raises an eyebrow. 'Are you sure that's the best approach?'

A: 'I mean, it seems easier. I don't want to hurt her feelings, you know?'

B: 'Ghosting may seem like the path of least resistance, but it can leave a trail of confusion and hurt feelings. Have you considered being upfront about your feelings instead?'

A: 'I guess I haven't thought about it. I just don't want to deal with the awkward conversation.'

---

[30] One-sided love.
[31] Reference to a famous dialogue from *Ae Dil Hai Mushkil* (2016),

B: 'It's understandable that those conversations can be uncomfortable, but honesty is generally the better policy. Ghosting can leave people with unanswered questions and make them feel disrespected.'

A: 'Yeah, I get that. I just don't want to be the bad guy.'

B: 'Being honest doesn't make you the bad guy. It shows respect for the other person's feelings and allows both of you to move on more smoothly. It's like ripping off a band-aid—it might sting at first, but it's better in the long run.'

Definition of ghosting: It is the sudden and unexplained cessation of communication by one person with another. In simpler terms, it's when a person abruptly ends all contact with someone they were dating or talking to, without any explanation or warning. The person who is 'ghosting' essentially disappears from the other person's life by ignoring calls, messages and any attempts at contact. This behaviour can be hurtful and confusing for the person who is being ghosted as they are left without closure or an understanding of what went wrong. Ghosting can occur at various stages of a relationship. From the early stages of getting to know someone to more established and serious connections.

Harshita speaks: *Teri bina kehke lenge!* (It will damage you without asking you!)

Scenario 10

A: 'So, what's the deal with friends with benefits and fuck buddies? Aren't they the same thing?'

B nods. 'Ah, casual connections. While both involve a level of intimacy, there are nuanced differences worth exploring.'

A: 'What makes friends with benefits different from fuck buddies?'

B: 'Let's start with Friends with Benefits (FWB). In this scenario, the emphasis is on the 'friends' part. You and your FWB have a baseline of friendship, even if it's just grabbing a coffee now and then or sharing a few laughs. The benefits part adds a dash of physical intimacy to the mix without jeopardizing the friendship.'

A: 'So, it's like having your cake and eating it too—a friendship with a side of romance?'

B: 'Exactly! Now, fuck buddies, on the other hand, are more straightforward. The connection revolves primarily around the physical aspect. It's less about sharing your deepest secrets and more about, well, the other benefits.'

A: 'So, no late-night heart-to-hearts with a fuck buddy?'

B: 'Not typically. Fuck buddies thrive on keeping it light and uncomplicated. It's more about enjoying the moment without delving into the intricacies of life.'

A: 'Got it. So, FWB involves a friendship foundation, and fuck buddies are more, well, benefits-oriented.'

B: 'Precisely. Make sure you and your casual companion are on the same page to avoid any unexpected plot twists. Always be clear about your boundaries and expectations.'

Harshita speaks: Friends are people you don't want to fuck around with; FWB are friends who you fuck up emotionally, physically, mentally and beyond. WOW.

Scenario 11

A: He was so sweet at first, but now he's manipulative and jealous all the time. I guess he love-bombed me.

B: 'What happened?'

A sighs. 'At the beginning, he was all charm and affection. It felt like I was floating on a cloud of compliments and attention. But now, it's like a switch flipped, and he's controlling and possessive. Love bombing is when someone showers you with affection and attention initially, but it often turns into controlling behaviour. It's like they create this intense emotional connection to gain influence.'

B: 'Now, it must be like walking on eggshells. It's tough when things change so dramatically. Have you talked to him about how you're feeling?'

A: 'I've tried, but every time I bring up my concerns, he dismisses them or gets defensive. It's like I'm not allowed to question anything.'

B: 'That's a red flag. Healthy relationships thrive on respect for each other's feelings. Love shouldn't feel like a cage.'

A: 'I'm starting to see that now. It's just hard because the person I fell for initially feels completely different from him.'

B: 'It's okay to prioritize your well-being. If the relationship is causing you distress, it might be worth reassessing whether it's a healthy environment for you. Remember, you deserve a

relationship built on trust, communication, and
mutual respect. Don't settle for less.'

Love bombing is manipulative behaviour in which
one person overwhelms another with excessive
affection, compliments, and expressions of love or
admiration, often in the early stages of a relationship.
The purpose is to create a sense of intense emotional
connection and dependency, making it easier for the
manipulator to control or exploit the other person.

Harshita speaks: Congratulations, you are in
love with a manipulator. Change him or else he'll
change you (not in a good way). *sigh*

Scenario 12

A: 'He only ever dates divorcees. He's a real
pie-hunter.'

B: 'That's a new one. What's that dating
preference?'

A: 'Well, it's like he has a radar for divorced
individuals. Every time he starts dating someone,
it turns out they've been through a divorce. It's
become a bit of a pattern.'

B: 'Erm?'

A: 'Exactly. It's like he's drawn to the seasoned slices of life. I started calling him a pie-hunter as a joke, but now I'm starting to wonder if there's a deeper reason.'

B: 'It's interesting how people develop preferences. Maybe he just appreciates people that come with life experiences.'

A: 'Could be. But sometimes, I wonder if he's intentionally seeking out complexity.'

B: 'Well, as long as everyone is a consenting adult and happy.'

A grinning. 'True, as long as it's a consensual pie-sharing arrangement. Who knew dating could be so much like a dessert menu?'

Definition of pie-hunter: A questionable dating trend involving an individual (the 'hunter') intentionally pursuing individuals, referred to as 'pies', who have experienced heartbreak or have complicated dating histories. These individuals are perceived as more susceptible and less demanding.

Harshita speaks: Love without a dessert . . . giver without a heart to give ... and poetry without a rhyme. Ewww, who wants that?

Scenario 13

A: 'So it turned out he'd been seeing like, six other girls the whole time!'

B: 'Damn. You got roached.'

A: 'Roached? What's that? Is it some new dating slang?'

B: 'Yeah, it's when someone you're dating turns out to be seeing multiple people simultaneously. You know, like roaches scatter when you turn on the lights—hidden relationships suddenly come crawling out.'

A groans. 'Ugh, the dating world is turning into a bug-infested nightmare. Who comes up with these terms?'

B laughs. 'Well, at least now you have a name for it. Roaching—a classic case of someone spreading their romantic wings far and wide.'

A: 'I thought we were exclusive! I had no idea he was building a whole romantic insectarium.'

B: 'Unfortunately, roaching is all too common these days. The important thing is that you found out and can move on from the insect farm.'

A: 'True. No more roaches for me. I'm upgrading to a butterfly garden.'

Definition of roaching: A term used in the context of dating and relationships to describe a situation where one person, while in a supposedly monogamous relationship, hides the fact that they are dating or romantically involved with other people. It implies a lack of transparency and honesty about one's dating activities, like hiding in the metaphorical 'roaches' or hidden corners of a relationship. Roaching often involves deceptive behaviour and can lead to trust issues when the truth is revealed.

Harshita speaks: Cheatified. *Dhokhafied*. *Gumrahfied*.[32] It is everything that infidelity is. Sorry (hugs).

Scenario 14

A: 'I had such a good time with Jake while he was home for the holidays, but he broke up with me as soon as he got back to campus.'

B: 'Classic Turkey dumped.'

A: 'Huh? Everything seemed great over the holidays. We even talked about making plans for

---

[32] Betrayed, manipulated.

Christmas. But as soon as he got back to campus, he hit me with the break-up talk.'

B: 'What went wrong?'

A: 'I have no idea. He said he needed space and wanted to focus on his studies. It felt like I went from being a feast to the leftovers he tossed in the fridge.'

B: 'The classic "it's not you, it's me" move. But seriously, who breaks up after such a cozy holiday?'

A laughs. 'I know, right? It's like he got his fill of turkey and decided he was done with the whole meal.'

B: 'Well, if he's not appreciating what you bring to the table, he's missing out. Turkey dumped or not, you deserve someone who values you.'

Definition of Turkey Dumped: Turkey dumped is a phrase that typically refers to a situation in which one party abruptly ends a romantic relationship with another person. It means that the relationship has been terminated by one party, often without warning or explanation, leaving the other person feeling hurt or rejected.

Harshita speaks: Leaving a love job without serving any notice period is what leaving others high and dry looks like. Would have been nice to cut them some slack at least!

Scenario 15

A: 'She won't introduce me to any of her friends or family. I think I'm being stashed.'

B: 'What's that supposed to mean?'

A: 'You know, when someone you're dating keeps you hidden away and doesn't introduce you to the important people in their life. It's like being stored away on a shelf, only brought out when convenient.'

B: 'Ah, I get it now. Stashed in the relationship storage, kept out of sight. That's not cool. Have you talked to her about it?'

A: 'I tried bringing it up, but she's always deflecting or changing the subject. It's like I'm in some secret compartment of her life.'

B: 'Sounds frustrating. A relationship should be a team effort, not a solo act with a secret player.'

A: 'Exactly! I want to be part of her life, not kept in the relationship shadows.'

B: 'Maybe it's time for a serious conversation about where you both see this going. If she's not willing to open up, you might need to reassess if this is the right relationship for you.'

Definition of stashed: It can be used to describe a situation where someone is keeping a romantic interest hidden or secret from others. For instance, if someone is romantically involved with someone else but has another person they're seeing on the side without the knowledge of the first person, you might say that the second person is 'stashed' away.

Harshita speaks: Don't be a Mastani to his Bajirao. Why put yourself through all the pain and trauma, when you deserve rain and marijuana (haha, kidding!)

FROM AC'S DESK

When the heart breaks and betrayal is involved, anger is one of the primary emotions we experience. And when it hurts, retaliation is almost our natural first instinct. Ancient Greek Tragedian Euripides in his famous text, *Medea*, wrote, 'Stronger than lover's love is lover's hate. Incurable, in each, the wounds they make.'[33]

But revenge is always a self-defeating idea in the long run and Shakespearean dramas are filled with such examples. As Confucius says, 'Before you embark on a journey of revenge, dig two graves.'

So why do we get so charged up to seek revenge? Well, because we believe that it will release the pent-up emotions within us, if we take some punitive actions, feel the catharsis of it and find closure. Very rarely does it pan out like that.

Interestingly, on the American Psychological Association website, author Michael Price talks of various research, across the years, while pointing out that revenge comes at a price and instead of

---

[33] Euripedes, 'Quotable Quote', Goodreads, https://www.goodreads.com/quotes/419-stronger-than-lover-s-love-is-lover-s-hate-incurable-in-each.

helping us to move on with our lives, it can leave us dwelling on the situation and remaining unhappy.[34]

While acceptance and forgiveness is the path everyone will advise you to take, these don't drop on you like a Newtonian Apple. It takes a lot of self-work to alchemize those aggressive feelings into a more productive one. So, how does one alchemize these jumbled-up feelings? You feel through your aggression, you doddle your pain, you journal your frustration, you make your memories, you paint your disappointment, you plant your loss (in the garden) and talk through your angst. You feel your feelings by actively engaging your body and integrating all those feelings with it. And it's a good time to reach out to a therapist and work with them as your put in the work. What might my alchemized feelings look like? To each his own, but for Chilean Poet and 1971 Nobel Prize Winner, Pablo Neruda, it looked something like this:

If You Stop Loving Me[35]

Well, now
If little by little you stop loving me
I shall stop loving you

---

[34] Michael Price, 'Revenge and the people who seek it', *Monitor on Psychology*, American Psychological Association, June 2009, https://www.apa.org/monitor/2009/06/revenge.

[35] *Selected Poems of Pablo Neruda* (UK: Vintage Classics, 2012).

Little by little
If suddenly you forget me
Do not look for me
For I shall already have forgotten you

Modern love is now viewed as a psychological landmine. One has to truly navigate, hop, step and jump to be able to keep oneself safe. Never before in the history of romantic relationships, dating or marriage, did people find themselves grappling with so many variables.

In the new world order, dating has become a series of complex social interactions, with a plethora of choices, which ideally should be helpful but has made finding 'the one' even more difficult. The landscape of relationships per se has evolved, leading to isolation, hiding behind the screen, new dating vocabulary, emotional fatigue, lack of commitment, attachment issues and a general sense of disillusionment about finding a partner for life. So often in my conversations with young people, I find them struggling with the rigmarole of finding, connecting, nurturing and maintaining a romantic relationship.

'What's your advice?' The three dreaded words that are thrown at me often. I wish I had a checklist to hand over, which can guarantee a successful dating pattern and long-term relationships. But instead, what I have is an acronym which may come in handy when you are going through the process. And that's P.A.C.E.

Priority, Authenticity, Communication, Empathy.

Priority: Prioritize the self. Who you are, what your value system is, who you are when no one's watching, your interests, hobbies, needs and desires. In a world which loves to glaze everything with a layer of compromise, I dare you to prioritize yourself. While it may sound like a counterproductive point as you read this, bear with me, as I try to explain this further.

Prioritizing the self involves knowing the self. And that requires work. Most of us would gingerly jump into relationships without any thought to who we truly are or what we truly want in a partner. In our haste to find someone for company, we often make the cardinal mistake of focusing on who is available and not who is compatible. Prioritizing oneself means recognizing things we want in a relationship and doing the due diligence with yourself. List your value system, make a list of your virtues, your work-in-progress spaces, your life goals and long-term dreams. These require extensive introspection, talking through, self-development and effort, but if you skip this step, you are likely to land in a relationship that will become a major challenge. Perhaps not the kind of dating hack you were looking for, but then, most romance novels lied. And if they didn't lie, they peddled a lot of unrealistic dreams in the name of poetic licence.

Authenticity: No one sums up authenticity like Shakespeare does in his play Hamlet. '....to thine own self be true, And it must follow, as the night the day, Thou canst not then be false to any man'. While we would all love to put our best foot forward in the first few months of the dating state, the masks wear off quickly. So, the more honest we are about our lives, the more chances of drawing in a partner who wants to be with us and not the illusion we create. Charm can only take you so far. When the veneer falls off, we all are flawed human beings with vulnerable parts. I will even go so far to say that you might as well show your true colours early, at least it guarantees your partner lesser negotiations, later.

Feels like the worst advice ever, right?

A relationship is an investment for your mind, body, soul and finances. Let your investment partner see as clearly as possible what they are getting into. Make your relationship an authentic partnership from the very beginning so that you give it all the life force you have to help it survive and thrive.

Communication (and comprehension): I write communication and comprehension together because they belong together. They can't yield results without each other. Whether you are dating or building a new relationship, communicating effectively with your partner is paramount. I can't express myself, I don't know how to talk about my feelings, I don't know how to address conflict are excuses of the past. With social media taking over our collective psyches, whether or not you like it, communication can no longer be compromised. Find your channel, of course; face-to-face talk, texting, calls, whatever works for you and your partner, but communication is key to the new world order. And given the technology-oriented world we live in and the hiding behind the screen fear we all grapple with, it's paramount that we put in efforts to communicate and develop the patience for our partner to comprehend us. Because you can communicate all you want, but without your partner comprehending what you meant, it is a colossal waste of time and effort.

Communicate consistently and as clearly as possible. Address conflicts as soon as possible and create space for comprehension and discussion as much as possible.

Empathy: Internet's favourite word! And a very useful tool to maintain long term relationships. Former US President Theodore Roosevelt had once famously said, 'No one cares how much you know, until they know how much you care.' The truth about empathy is, it's not commonly found, although it's talked about a lot. The ability to understand, see things from the point of view of a different person and to imagine yourself in their place, are not easy tasks. We might sympathize, but true empathy isn't easy.

We all are adults wrestling with our childhood conditioning, and this itself is the reason why both partners need empathy and compassion towards the adults they have become. Empathy towards your partner helps them feel seen and validated, which can go a long way in developing emotional intimacy. Long-term relationships will need you to keep accessing your empathetic parts, especially when you both are addressing a conflict. In fact, it can become the cornerstone of the partnership and once your companion is secure in terms of feeling understood, they are likely to extend the same grace to you. Empathy is therapeutic, try it.

So, when in doubt, PACE it out.

8

Chee Chee, Sex Bola[36]

So, the ever-so-elusive discussion on sex has been a tad overdue. We spoke about love, heartbreaks, tears, different kinds of relationships and first kisses. But *hawwwww*, sex *ke baare mein kaise*? (How do we talk about sex?)

But staying true to the obstinate rebel I am, who always does exactly what she is advised against, it was imperative that I wrote about the one thing Indians love to do (we crossed China in population this year), are good at it (Kamasutra et. al.) but hate to discuss (explains the population).

So, all you *sati savitris*,[37] shed your *sharam*[38] and let's go?

Our perception of sex is woven from the threads of our relationship with our bodies. It stems from

---

[36] Disgusting! He said 'sex'.
[37] Chaste women.
[38] Honour.

168

somewhere between self-awareness and societal expectations. From the moment we become conscious of our physical form, our sense of self is inextricably linked to the vessel that carries us through life—our body. How we navigate this complex terrain profoundly influences our attitudes toward sex.

Society, with its kaleidoscope of standards and expectations, often casts a long shadow upon our self-perception. The mirror becomes a silent arbiter, reflecting not only our physical attributes, but also the expectations placed upon us. In this delicate dance, we may find ourselves scrutinizing every curve, every imperfection, as if our worth were measured in pixels and proportions.

Now this section is more for our female readers, but I promise you the knowledge will only sensitize the men. Women, let's talk about the orgasm you never had . . .

Now, you didn't think I was going to begin this with anything else besides discussing the orgasm gap between men and women, did you? This gap often lurks in the shadows, leaving many women in the dark about the joy of a happy ending.

I have often wondered about the whys and here's what I have deduced:

1. The void of sexual education: In a world where sexual education is a cryptic puzzle missing from the curriculum, many Indian women navigate their intimate terrain without a map, clueless about their own bodies and the pleasure they can potentially have. They spend most of their lives awaiting its discovery and sadly enough, many never discover it.

2. Cultural shush-hush stigmas: Cultural taboos weave a tangled web, ensnaring discussions about pleasure. Openly talking about satisfaction becomes an act shrouded in stigma, leaving women hesitant to voice their desires. Men openly talk about being dissatisfied and how their partners and wives have chronic headaches, but no one ever stopped and asked the ladies what was causing the headaches.

3. Gender inequality unveiled: The gender roles and inequalities add another layer to this complex narrative. In a society where expectations often outweigh exploration, women might find themselves on a tightrope, balancing their partner's satisfaction while their desires go unnoticed.

4. The enigma of female sexual agency: The patriarchal set-up is a world where women hold the keys to their pleasure kingdom but feel disempowered to use them. Traditional

norms can stifle agency, turning sexual exploration into a clandestine affair and preventing women from fully expressing their desires.

5. Culture clash and religious influences: Cultural and religious threads weave into the sexual fabric, shaping attitudes and beliefs. Conservative ideals cast a shadow on open conversations about pleasure, leaving women in the dark about the profound importance of their own orgasmic experiences. For instance (Haww! alert), try having sex during periods. Go with an open mind; it's the right kind of bloodbath.

6. The silent language barrier: The reluctance to openly communicate desires, preferences and concerns with each other often turns the intimacy into a muted performance. In this quietness, both individuals long for a shared understanding, a connection that remains just out of reach in the unspoken spaces between them.

7. The clitoral conundrum: Research whispers a secret that society sometimes forgets—many women need clitoral stimulation to unlock the gates of ecstasy. Yet, the emphasis on penetrative prowess as the main event can lead to a missed memo, leaving women longing for the right touch.

8. The quest for pleasure: Limited access to sexual health services, including information on sexual pleasure and well-being, may contribute to the orgasm gap. Comprehensive sexual health education and resources can empower women to understand their bodies and sexual response.

Bridging the orgasm gap in India requires work; it demands a revolution that won't come with one movie. Btw, the 2023 release, *Thank you for Coming,* was a commendable effort towards starting the dialogue. But the revolution needs an evolution of sexual education, a dismantling of cultural taboos and a celebration of equality and communication. Let's strive to turn the tide, creating a world where the pursuit of pleasure is not targeted to men alone. Let the girls have some fun, please.

Sexual shame often arises from the discord between values and our personal beliefs. This misalignment prompts the unsettling question: 'Am I normal?' Unfortunately, when the answer seems to be 'no, I am not normal', it gives birth to shame—a feeling of flaw, brokenness, or being inherently bad.

Let's examine a few things I can think of:

1. Spontaneous desire is sexy—umm is it humanly possible?
2. Ejaculatory control is good sex—not necessarily; stop being a bunny rabbit without climax in sight.
3. Men must be able to achieve and maintain erections—It's a plus, but again, hold the girl instead. Goes a long way!
4. Women achieve orgasms through intercourse—ask around and you'll know.
5. Sexual problems are easily fixable—inaccurate. Usually, they fester until a break-up.
6. 36DD is the ideal boob size. 10 inches is the ideal penis size—size doesn't matter as long you know how to use it well.
7. Naked bodies should conform to certain standards—stop using porn as a reference.
8. Masturbation should be unnecessary in a relationship—there is nothing called enough pleasure.
9. Intercourse should be daily and relentless—Stop watching *Animal* (2023).
10. Fantasy is unnecessary in a sexual relationship—dreams are never bad.
11. Men should take the lead sexually—a woman in charge can be sexy. Try it, ladies!

Before you overthink it and blame your inherent sense of badness, hear me out:

1. Premarital sex is NOT a sin; sexual compatibility is crucial to marriage.
2. Casual sexual behaviour, particularly in women, is NOT promiscuity.
3. Watching porn is NOT bad.
4. Being LGBTQ+ is NOT a sin.
5. Paying for sex is your discretion, but just remember sexual exploitation and sex trafficking are real things. It is not a moral judgement, it's a social cause you must remember.
6. Masturbation is NOT bad.
7. Casual or anonymous sex is NOT bad.
8. Kink is NOT perverted; polyamory is NOT immoral.

Talking about sex openly helps you work on your shame—because honestly, it's better to tackle those awkward conversations now than to find out your idea of 'foreplay' was actually a game of Twister!

You must work on your shame. Here's how:

1. Don't hide; work on it. People withdraw or hide from the situation, experiencing sadness, fear and anxiety. For instance, someone

facing erectile dysfunction may retreat from dating and intimacy, abandoning romantic aspirations due to despair and anxiety.

2. What's with the self-hate? People turn anger inward, directing it towards themselves. This response involves self-labelling and furious self-criticism. For example, someone feeling shame around masturbation may label themselves a sex addict, striving for total abstinence and engaging in self-punishment when failing to meet their exacting standards.

3. People attempt to circumvent shame by dissociating from negative feelings associated with it. For instance, instead of working on a bad sex life, people divert attention to work or exercise.

4. Blaming someone else is easier. This helps you from not working on yourself. Sex workers in Thailand will tell you stories of their customers blaming their partner for neglecting their sexual needs, portraying themselves as a victim.

In therapy, the focus is on understanding the context and root of shame, the self-beliefs it generates and the defences employed. Cope with it, and hopefully, with a wonderful partner, it will be better.

In season 4, episode 11 of *Friends*, titled 'The One with Phoebe's Uterus', Monica teaches Chandler about the seven erogenous zones on a woman's body. This is a fictional and humorous scene from a sitcom but has some strands of truth. The concept of erogenous zones varies from person to person, and there is no strict scientific basis for the specific number or locations of erogenous zones.

In the show, Monica draws a diagram for Chandler to illustrate the seven zones.

While the concept of zones is subjective and can vary from person to person, here's a general list of some areas that are commonly considered sensitive and pleasurable for many individuals.

Keep in mind that preferences can differ and communication with your partner is essential to understand their specific desires and boundaries. Also, it's important to approach any intimate activities with respect and consent.

- Lips: Gentle kissing and nibbling on the lips can be pleasurable.
- Neck: The neck is often a sensitive area. Kissing, licking, or softly blowing on the neck can be arousing.
- Ears: Whispering, gentle kisses, or nibbling on the earlobes can be quite stimulating.
- Breasts and Nipples: Many women find stimulation of the breasts and nipples to be

pleasurable. This can involve gentle caresses, kisses, or more focused attention.

- Inner thighs: The inner thighs are a sensitive area that can respond well to gentle touching or kissing.
- Lower back: Light caresses or massages on the lower back can be relaxing and sensual.
- Clitoris: The clitoris is a highly sensitive area for many women and is often a key focus for sexual pleasure. Techniques can include gentle stroking, licking, or oral stimulation.

There you go, and as Monica rightly advised, mix them up and keep them on their toes.

Go for a 1, 2, 1, 2, 3, 3, 5, 4, 3, 2, 2, a 2, 4, 6, 2, 4, 6, 4, 2, 2, 4, 7, 5, 7, 6, 7, 7, 7 ... and ... Woohoo!

The rollercoaster ride of first-time sexual escapades is like trying to assemble IKEA furniture without instructions—exciting, nerve-wracking and you're not entirely sure if you're doing it right. The air is thick with anticipation and the room is charged with enough awkward energy to power a small city.

Picture this: you and your partner, armed with the collective knowledge of a few movies and some questionable advice from your more 'experienced' friends, decide to take the plunge. Spoiler alert: it's not going to be graceful.

Suddenly, you find yourselves performing a dance routine that neither of you practised. Because real-life intimacy doesn't come with a director yelling 'cut' and a team of makeup artists waiting in the wings.

And let's not forget the unrealistic expectations. Thanks to movies, we've been conditioned to believe that our first time should be a seamless, choreographed masterpiece. But it's more like a blooper reel—one where you're the star, director and audience, all at once.

The pressure to perform is real, folks. It's like being on a cooking show with Gordon Ramsay as the judge. Only instead of critiquing your risotto, he's critiquing your ability to execute a perfect dismount. No pressure, right?

Lack of communication is the reason for this comedy of errors. It's like playing a game of charades, but instead of guessing movie titles, you're trying to decipher your partner's mysterious signals. It's not as fun as it sounds.

But within the awkwardness lies the potential for hilarity and genuine connection. Those fumbles and missteps? They're the unexpected plot twists that make the story uniquely yours. Embrace the awkwardness, laugh off the pressure and revel in the fact that your love story is an original, not a poorly executed remake.

In the scheme of things, first-time awkwardness is the first step of intimacy. It might feel a bit wobbly at first, but it's a crucial step towards the adventures that await. So, here's to embracing the awkward, navigating the uncharted with a sense of humour and discovering the joy in the beautifully imperfect symphony of first-time experiences. After all, who said intimacy couldn't come with a side of laughter and a generous sprinkle of awkward charm?

Let's face it, when it comes to getting down and dirty, it's not just about the physical bit; it's a full-blown emotional act.

On your first night together with your partner, it's not just about the what-goes-where logistics; it's about navigating a minefield of feelings, expectations and the occasional existential crisis.

Now, emotional preparedness is key to sex. You're not sure what's ahead, but you've got to trust that your emotional GPS won't lead you straight into a tree. It's about being ready for the emotional ride.

Emotional vulnerability is like a superhero costume—powerful, slightly uncomfortable and something you wouldn't wear to a casual brunch. Being emotionally prepared means strapping on that cape and accepting that vulnerability is not a weakness but a damn superpower. You must shed all that baggage of the past to be present for another person today. By then, I hope there's enough investment in it to make it enjoyable for both.

Trust, my dear readers, is the secret sauce of any successful intimate endeavour. It's the glue that holds together the delicate Jenga tower of emotions and nakedness. Without trust, it's like trying to build a sandcastle in a hurricane.

Now, let's talk about the impact of emotional unpreparedness. It's like attempting to parallel park without ever taking a driving lesson—anxiety-inducing, prone to accidents and likely to leave a dent in your emotional bumper.

Be your best, embrace your emotional side and build trust like it's Fort Knox.

Being emotionally ready isn't just a tip; it's your ticket to a satisfying ride. Get set for a wave of feelings and remember—emotions aren't on the sidelines; they're the main event of the intimacy journey. Stay invested.

Imagine a night where the air is charged with anticipation and two souls are on the brink of a journey together. This isn't just any evening; it's a special one. You know it even before it happens; there is a connection, laughter, emotion and desire—the kind that lingers in the heart long after the night has faded into memory.

Let's break it down into four steps for you to understand better:

Step 1: The Great Date: A Prelude to Something More

The evening begins with a date that feels like a stolen moment from a dream. Maybe it's a cozy dinner by candlelight where laughter and shared glances weave an invisible thread between two people. Or perhaps it's a moonlit escapade where every whispered word adds to the electric charge in the air. I will tell you mine—a 3 a.m. walk on a beach followed by conversation that wouldn't end till morning. It was that day when I realized that a date is not just to impress but to create an atmosphere where hearts sync, setting the stage for the unveiling of something extraordinary.

Step 2: Foreplay: Touch and Tenderness

Foreplay isn't a checklist; it's about hands exploring, lips lingering and gazes speaking volumes. It's in the subtleties, the glances that speak of longing and the gentle touches that convey a hunger for more. In these moments, time seems to stretch, creating a space where every caress and whispered desire builds a bridge between two people. It's a prelude, heightening the senses and forging a connection that goes beyond the physical.

Step 3: Asking Consent

I was taken aback when Shrey asked me if he could kiss me for the first time. We are rarely accustomed to someone understanding boundaries. But with Shrey, I learnt the value of something as basic as a yes. The fact that he asked reflected his respect towards me and his own feelings. Our desires align and that consent becomes an affirmation of trust and respect. It's not a formality but a mutual agreement. In these words, vulnerability meets understanding, and there is an acknowledgement of boundaries. Consent isn't just a word; it's a promise.

Step 4: The Grand Act

And then, the crescendo—the grand act where pleasure is not a destination but a journey. Bodies become a canvas and every touch is a stroke of ecstasy. It's a celebration of intimacy where the goal is the sheer joy of giving and receiving pleasure. Focus on each other—on discovering the nuances.

In the aftermath, as you lie entwined in the afterglow, indulge in some post-care. Affectionate whispers, tender embraces and jokes become the echoes of a time where vulnerability and pleasure merged into something profoundly personal.

A perfect erotic evening is a memory that lingers in the spaces between heartbeats.

Alright, listen up, lovebirds! When it comes to getting cozy in the bedroom, we need to talk about the warning signs. If your partner's idea of consent is as clear as mud, we've got a problem. Consent isn't a riddle; it's a straightforward conversation. If things feel confusing, hit the brakes! Healthy relationships thrive on open communication and respect, not mysterious signals. Remember, consent is an ongoing discussion, not a one-time handshake. If you catch a vibe of discomfort or hesitation, it's time for a pit stop. Ignoring these red flags isn't just uncool; it's a recipe for disaster. So, in romance, make sure your signal is always crystal clear, because murky waters are for pirates, not partners!

Here are some red flags no one told you about:

1. If he doesn't care about your pleasure and what you like in bed, get rid of him immediately.

2. Don't be forced, coerced or manipulated into doing something you don't want to do. *Ek baar karke toh dekho? Nahi karna hai?* (Let's give it a try? Not interested?) Move on.

3. Just like women, men aren't always in the mood. It's okay for both parties to say no to sex on a given day. It is neither about the health of the relationship nor about the loss of interest. He is just not in the mood and that's okay too.

4. Sex is not a band-aid for your problems. Make-up sex is hot, but it doesn't solve your problems.

5. If someone gets you drunk to have sex, run for your life. This is never going to be anything besides a terrible hangover.

6. If he or she has an STI, and you don't know about it—it is shabby. Just plain shabby.

7. Don't compare the moves with your ex-lovers'. It's not nice!

8. Guilting your partner into sex is a despicable move

9. If they point out scars, marks, your fat, or pigmentation of your body, they need to be dumped right away.

10. Aggression of any form is a strict NO. Unless you like it wild and it's consensual.

Bouncing back from the seven-year itch*

Seven years into a marriage and people are not just itching; they are practically ready to bounce. But let's help you guys add items from your bucket list.

Who knew the seven-year itch could be the catalyst for a marital adventure?

Let's talk about spicing things up . . . This part of the chapter is your guide to breaking the routine and shaking things up in the bedroom. Embrace the fun, ditch the dull and let your imagination run wild.

After all, the only thing better than a routine romp is a night of surprises that even your favourite Netflix show can't compete with!

Let's go:

1. Experiment with sex lives—sexy lingerie and a diverse range of toys. Beat the monotony!

2. Don't stop talking to each other about what you enjoy in bed. Ask for things that are risque or left unspoken. Keep communication lines open and be clear about what is working and not working in bed.

3. Roleplay your way through adventure. Act like you are meeting for the first time all over again, every few months. The high of the first time needs to be relieved to keep the sex enticing.

4. Live your fantasies, help your partner make it happen. Have sex on the beach, on conference tables, public bathrooms, on a flight. Fantasies are meant to be illogical, and your partner must match your madness.

5. Consult a counsellor or doctor, especially in older couples. Don't shy away from discussing issues that are bound to crop up sooner or later. And don't let those make you sign up for a life of abstinence. Age has nothing to do with libido! Be happy bunnies.

FROM AC'S DESK

Our body needs to heal from heartbreaks.

Relationship break-ups can be torturous, and we often feel it viscerally in our chest, in our head, our throat and our gut. The neurology behind heartbreak reveals an interesting interplay between our brains, bodies and emotions during this period of acute stress.

Our bodies learn to co-regulate when we live in such proximity with our partners. Several research has pointed towards the fact that a couple's overall well-being improves in a stable relationship. While sexual intimacy isn't the only marker for a healthy relationship, it is an important one. A safe, consensual and active sex life can help lower stress, ease anxiety, boost our immune system and enhance our mood. Orgasms are known to bathe the body with happy hormones which helps with muscle relaxation.

Sex isn't just an act of the body; the mind is also equally involved. The simple act of being close to your partner and touching and hugging during sex can strengthen the bond between two people.

When this connection is interrupted, our bodies can feel thrown off and abandoned in many ways. One might feel a lot of fear, sadness, and confusion due to the distance and hostility that follows most break-ups.

On the other hand, our physical longings may draw us back to the familiar arms of the former partner. Also, the push and pull within us to quickly find someone new or wait it out can cause a lot of psychological distress.

This transition period is hard on the body and the mind but it is crucial to take time off from dating and heal from the break-up. This is an important period in one's life. It's a time for assessing what went wrong, recognizing our patterns, if any, understanding how we might have played a role in the breakdown of the relationship and reflecting on the various aspects of partnership.

Our self-esteem may feel bruised after a break-up, and we may question our worth. Many aspects of our selfhood feel compromised, when we are fresh out of a relationship that brought us a lot of pain. It's advisable to step back completely from dating for a while and spend time and resources finding, nurturing and caring for our selfhood.

It's important to view this period as a life transition and invest in somatic therapy such as dance movement sessions, sound therapy, breathwork, art-based sessions, and meditation retreats which can do us a world of good. The emotional and physical release of pent-up thoughts and emotions must happen; in whatever way we can access it.

9

Bhaisaab, Meri Shaadi Ho Gayi[39]

For a long time, Shrey and I didn't tell anyone about us. He and I dated for more than two years but for the first two years, we didn't tell people except our close family and friends. People jinx things. It was perhaps our best move. Don't go public until it's permanent. Make your relationship so solid that when the barrage of people come your way with their opinions, judgement and advice, you can face it together.

But like I told you, romcoms don't quite tell you what happens after the curtains fall on the film once the hero and heroine have had their grand kiss.

What follows is a lot of bargaining—*na tera, na mera, beech mein done kartey hai* (Neither your way nor my way, let's come to the middle ground). Philosophers call it mutual understanding; parents

---

[39] Brother, I got married.

call it compromise; I simply call it the equalizing phase of a relationship where my partner and I actively work towards meeting each other halfway.

The day after Shrey and I kissed for the first time, I sat him down and had a serious chat. 'I don't do flings,' I said 'If I love, I love and I like going all the way in love,' I told him clearly.

I knew right from the start that this was a relationship for keeps. There was this fire between us after that kiss. Until then, we were meeting, chilling and that's it. Kissing was a big deal, for me. I was always very protective of my body's energy, and I didn't believe in kissing random frogs. In that first kiss, I knew Shrey was someone I wanted for a long time in my life. I was a damaged person falling in love and so I was utterly petrified to imagine that this could be forever. But yes, I knew this had the makings of a relationship that could last a lifetime.

We were hugging while lying in bed that night. I was thinking of too many things all at once. And the most prominent thought in my mind was that I had a lot of love to give, but I knew I wouldn't survive another heartbreak. I still remember what I told Shrey after that: 'There is a spark between us. It's almost electrifying. This can go right. I am looking for a partner and hoping to marry that person. So, if you are someone who isn't at the same place as me, you should leave and never come back again.'

If we kept meeting, I knew I would lose my heart to him. My feelings would get stronger with time. Wary of another heartbreak, I didn't want to choose pain. So, I made it clear.

Relationships are about love, sure; but they are also about timing and one's own headspace. Timing is everything. If it is not your time, it won't work out.

Luckily, Shrey was in the same place as I. We weren't sure if it would lead to marriage, but it was worth giving it a shot. For any relationship to make it in the long run, it is necessary that both people be on the same page. Don't believe romcoms that tell you confused men are cute. You saw what happened to me and the not-adorable-at-all confused chap.

Young people falling in love, just know that it is best to be straight with the person you are with about what you are looking for with them. Don't hurt them or take them for a ride. Don't play petty games. By the time we get through our twenties, we are done and drained with relationships that have probably wrung us dry. We have had a few heartbreaks, godawful dates and figured out what we are seeking. Remember to be clear about intentions.

When Shrey and I began our relationship, I thought it would be a romcom—balloons and flowers, long drives and dates and trips and treks. You get the drift. But no one tells you how difficult it is to build the foundation of a building. It is the hardest part. Most relationships fall through in the first year because of people's inability to navigate each other's headspace.

I soon discovered that Shrey and I are poles apart. My love language is physical touch. I want to meet every day, hug every day, and be around him every day. Shrey believes in space. If you don't see him for a month, he'd be okay with that. He didn't need to see my face to be in love with me. This was the toughest barrier in the first few weeks. I would try to meet and he'd be too lazy to come to my place. Our homes were far away from each other. In all my past relationships, I was used to men who'd physically be around. These were men who had no professional ambitions and were not working towards a goal. So, they were comfortable whiling away their time with me. But not Shrey, he was disciplined. He went to work every day and had a routine. In the beginning, his schedule didn't have enough room for me.

The logical woman inside me was incredibly proud of me for choosing well. For the first time in my life, I chose a man who was obsessed with life and growth instead of being obsessed about me. He had ambitions and wanted to build a life. Shrey had a lot to do in life. He didn't make his relationship his whole life. But behind every logical person is a needy kid who can't have enough of the good things they've been given. I probably got clingy. And for good reason.

I wasn't meeting Shrey quite enough. And a large part of why it was such is because of the situation in his family.

Shrey met me at a time in his life when he had just gone through a storm. A month before we met, Shrey lost his father. It was rather sudden. He got Covid and didn't make it, unfortunately. Losing a parent leaves behind a grief that can never be repaired. Now, I could hear the pain, but I didn't get it entirely. It took me a long time to fathom Shrey's trauma from losing his father so suddenly. Initially, I had a selfish approach—why should my relationship suffer? I wanted the dates and drives, and I wouldn't budge. I would either get angry or very passive-aggressive because I didn't see it as my problem to deal with. I had a figure-it-out dude approach.

Shrey met my abrasiveness with empathy. He talked it out with me every time there was the slightest insecurity or some small conflict. And I was a lot more pliant than I have ever been. I was willing to make dramatic shifts. By the time I met Shrey, I had been in therapy for long enough to know my patterns. Earlier, I would look for men who were as funny as me or as silly as me. But that's hardly the yardstick to make a life with. But Shrey was a guy who wanted a partner. He wanted to build a career and a life together, buy a dining table together and make a home together. We knew we had to meet each other halfway. We settled the primary conflict of our relationship by agreeing to meet each other twice a week.

Good bargain, I'd say.

The reason behind him not meeting me enough was left unresolved. It was Mummy—Shrey's mother. He couldn't leave his mother alone for very long and preferred spending most of his available time at home with her. I must blame Hindi soaps like *Tu Tu Main Main* for making me believe that mothers-in-law are demonic creatures. I have seen plenty of mothers-in-law who are plain villains. That coupled with the fact that Indian men have strange equations with their mothers and quite often, they become a reason for marital discord, was enough to make alarm bells ring.

I was weaving a narrative in my head based on facts. For the first six months, I couldn't go out on an elaborate date because he always had to rush back home. He didn't stay over because his mother was alone at home. I was worried about the very little time we spent together. How do you build anything when there is no time with each other? I was insecure in the first few months.

I somehow put two and two together and made it bigger than it should've been. I will let you decide if it was warranted or not. But I did a bit of mental math and realized I sacrificed too many things—a late-night drive, a movie date, a vacation together and sleepovers. These were small requests which couldn't be met. We met for three hours a week over two days. The needy girlfriend in me was at my wit's end.

Most of our early fights were around him not being able to let his mom stay alone. I didn't get it. I saw her as a third wheel in our relationship. I was very worried that he was possibly a Mumma's Boy, and that I would have to be around a clingy mother-in-law.

Six months into our relationship, I picked up a huge fight and told him off. 'If this is the best you can do, then let's not.' I wasn't okay with my needs not being met. I hated begging for my basics and I was incapable of asking for what I wanted. I needed physical presence a lot. Shrey's past relationships were different. It didn't matter if his previous partners were okay with it or not, I was not. We were two strong headed people in a relationship. Either it was going to be a mess, or something really beautiful.

Shrey knew rigidity couldn't move us forward. He relented and then, I did too.

The beautiful thing about Shrey is that he understood my standpoint completely. He didn't defend himself. He never once rubbished my feelings. He took on a lot of the balancing on his shoulders and made sure that my feeling antagonized by his mother was his responsibility and he was willing to fix it.

I guess the biggest learning comes from the most heightened and dramatic fight. He started making efforts. And effort, my friends, is a wonderful thing. It's something couples should never stop making. From the first six months and one major fight, I realized two things. Verbalize your wants and needs. Your partner isn't a magician who can know your unspoken words. Movie nights were a big deal for him; cooking was a big deal for me. For me, it's the smaller things that matter. The definition of romance differs from person to person. You don't always need to match each other's energy levels. He loved napping at home, I loved going out. He was a homebody who loved to laze around; I was the spontaneous one who wanted to be taken on a drive at 2 a.m. Determine your love language and know how far away it is from your partner's. That's the first step towards bridging the gap.

What happened to me in my past relationships made me guard my feelings and my heart. It was difficult on some days because I wouldn't relent. I wanted to follow a rulebook where I would be an equal giver and receiver of affection. But relationships aren't so neatly measured all the time. Some days, I worked hard and on other days, he did. I was in therapy during this phase because I was nearly sure that this wouldn't work. I was almost sure we would fail when Shrey assumed the responsibility of being the matured one of the two—he moved things around, set boundaries where needed and set out to build a life with me. He was sure that this was worth it.

After I noticed Shrey trying, I started breathing again. He convinced me to stay on. When you have stayed in toxic relationships repeatedly, being in a healthy one seems abnormal. There was a lot of undoing and unlearning needed. I needed to be reminded over and over again that I didn't need to be all caged up. I could finally relax. I had to give up my habit of overthinking.

With Aman, I had poured my all into the relationship. I had nothing left to give to Shrey. It was tricky for me as well. My instinct was to get riled up because of my trauma. But at the same time, the good person inside me would constantly say— don't be a bitch!

Aman had fucked me up to the point that trusting Shrey was hard. But I had to give it to him, he calmed me down in ways I didn't understand. After every fight, he would come over and simply talk. He knew all my words were coming from a deeper place. Like, I had to clearly tell him that his mother makes me insecure; I had to clearly state all my insecurities.

Shrey didn't take any of it badly at all. In fact, he understood that I wanted my personal space and time. He balanced it out over time. He kept assuring me that he would never choose his mother over me; and it felt like I had finally found a man who knows his mind.

He didn't make me feel stupid; he wasn't offended. Shrey is an evolved man who knows how to take care of his partner.

It was wonderful how we moulded ourselves to love each other the way we wanted to be loved. His sensitivity, warmth and kindness made me swoon. I was impressed with what a green flag he was. Love is the starting point but to keep the romance going, one needs to keep trying every day.

With Shrey, I learnt something profound about long-term relationships—it works because of intentions.

Within the first year, we had a lot of fights and dealt with some major conflicts. I disagree with people who say that fights weaken a relationship. Fights are essential to establish flaws and patterns, understand boundaries and know the value of compromise. Conflict resolution is key to determining how the relationship will pan out.

Conversations were our way of resolving conflicts. It mostly went like:

1. Okay, tell me what's wrong?
2. Is there anything more to this?
3. Are you frequently feeling this, or it is a one-off?
4. Hear me out.
5. I am sorry we had a terrible evening. But learning curve, right?

I knew Shrey was a green flag because he helped me work on becoming a better person. Of the numerous things he helped me navigate, the most significant one was his support in addressing my temper issues. When I am angry, I yell. I might not say mean things, but the decibels are high. I knew this was a problem, but it didn't dawn on me how much of a problem it was until I saw the impact it had on him. Did I want to change this about myself?

It's true that I have never loved anyone as much as I have loved Shrey. He would be impacted a lot by the yelling. There were days when I'd bring the house down with my shouting. After those yelling sessions, he would sit me down and tell me he hated how ugly I made fights. I saw the sincerity with which he told me this. There wasn't any grouse towards me, just concern. He wasn't being patronizing; he was simply saying, 'This bothers me a lot so please dial it down a bit.'

For the first time in my life, I could see how I was hurting people I love, especially Shrey, who would go to great lengths to prioritize my happiness over everything else. He made me want to change. I started taking anger management sessions.

I am learning ways to control my temper. Even today, I shout sometimes but I have learnt ways to work on this.

Usually, during a fight, I would extract myself from the equation, isolate myself and then calm down before having a conversation.

The infamous rage of Harshita Gupta is now reserved for Instagram reels of SoHarshi.

Within a year, our parents met. They liked each other and we decided to make the relationship official with a *roka*.[40] The permanence did good for us!

A month after our roka, I took Shrey to Dubai and proposed to him on top of the world (literally so). It was an elaborate thing I planned at the Burj

---

[40] Start of the courtship period.

Khalifa. I went down on my knees and proposed to my man. Well, he blushed and, of course, said yes!

Things moved rather quickly after that.

Now, no one prepares you for the changes that take place before marriage. I vacated the flat I was sharing with my friend and moved back to Lucknow. We had to be in a long-distance relationship until the wedding. Shrey never needed physical meetings to be in love, but I was all about the meetings. I couldn't go a whole month without meeting him.

How many staycations could we take? For the period leading up to our wedding, he came to meet me every alternate month. We were initially very worried about how we would navigate this. But things just kept getting easier.

It was almost as if the universe destined for us to have everything in order. But for the eight months, when we were not physically together, we grew emotionally closer as a couple. Through wedding monstrosities, couples lose perspective of why they are doing it at all amidst the noise and chaos.

In those moments, he handled my cold feet every time with a lot of care and tenderness. Every move he made was with me in mind. He stood by me, took small stands for me and gave me the lead in every decision. When I met Shrey, I was broken, but his love made me whole again.

While I handled my personal life, my professional life thrived. When the dark clouds move out, good things flow in by the bulk. But there are pros and very many cons of being famous.

People were unusually curious about who the person in my life was. And because we worked together and were repped by the same agency, we decided to keep it quiet.

During the phase when people were constantly asking me who the man in my life was, Shrey and I had elaborate conversations. Some very uncomfortable talks about success, failure and even money. We wanted to create an equitable marriage where we would share the load monetarily and emotionally. Also, we had to discuss how we would navigate the fact that I was doing better than him in my career at this point. Patriarchal societies don't know how to make sense of successful women, and so they don't let men breathe when they are with such women. Shrey and I had long conversations about the fragility of the male ego, and how we both can chew it and have a good laugh.

I can't say this enough, but insecurity is not an attractive virtue in men. Being comfortable in your skin is. Men, make the transition, please.

When people found out about us, there was a lot of chatter. The good thing was that we have never let the world come between us and that's why we won. We are strong together and I have never let people's words hamper Shrey's peace and vice versa. Shrey is a precious human being. Ever since I have fallen for him, I have had this instinct to protect him with every bit of strength I have.

Before Shrey, I had routinely been around men who saw my career as a hobby or 'time pass'. I was told—take the money you earn from us, we have lots. My father would be told that his girl couldn't work after marriage. The concept that I want to work hard to earn money was unimaginable to some of them. And then came Shrey, with his open heart, big arms and the best hug in the world to make me believe that my dreams matter, my hopes are real, and he will be with me through it all. He was the only man who didn't want to snatch away my individuality from me.

My success is as much his as it is mine. Men and women, especially women, choose someone who isn't afraid to let you shine. Never forget to have the uncomfortable conversations that you fear having. With the right partner, it only helps in making the relationship smoother.

Both of us were sure from the start that we wanted to get married, but Shrey hadn't proposed to me yet. Under the pretext of shooting a reel, he whisked me off to Bali. I was making boyfriend reels and fans wanted a reveal. So, this was the elaborate reveal video shoot we thought would be fun for the page.

People think everything in a public figure's life is orchestrated. Perhaps. But when you marry a man like Shrey, expect to be pleasantly surprised and, on some days, be swept off your feet. We went to Diamond Beach in Bali for a sunrise shoot. We reached the location at 5.30 a.m. For the first thirty minutes, the photographers, who were in on the plan, helped me with random shoots. At the brink of dawn, Shrey went down on his knees and proposed to me with a ring that had a butterfly and a pearl—I am a butterfly who likes adventures and he is my peace haven at the end of my antics. 'Will you marry me?' Shrey asked. It felt like the sun's glow shone on our relationship. It was the most perfect moment of my life and I teared up. I felt like the luckiest woman in the world.

Bad dates taught me that mediocre men will show up at my doorstep only because I have money, am successful and have social currency. They came to be with SoHarshi. The other breed were men who got intimidated fast. They either become fanboys or straight-up creepy. Then there was a third kind, who thought of me as a '*moti* party'.[41] Being famous has pros and cons. But with Shrey, I saw his intentions as pure. He was okay with earning less than me.

---

[41] Well-off people.

He didn't let the male ego come between us. He didn't care for the social media fandom and the frills of my life. He cared for the person I am. He was prepared to let my heightened emotions take a lot out of him. Remember the ring—calm to my storm!

I don't think dreams should come true; sometimes life has something grander in store and may that find its way to you.

I have seen grooms who look at wedding preparations as a liability. They leave it to their brides to carry the load, logistically and emotionally. And then, of course, the bride gets labelled bridezilla because of the volume of work and the sheer magnitude of the life shift that overwhelmed her. But not Shrey. He was with me like an equal partner should be. He was the one who made the mood board. He locked the venue after consulting me. We decided on the clothes we would wear. Everything was us, together.

And imagine a groom who'd fight the world to make your whims come true. Shrey was that groom, that husband. He did everything in his power to make sure that my dog Coco could be a part of our wedding celebrations. My father was against it and he had some valid reasons. We got married in the hills near a national forest (Jim Corbett). There was a lake next to the venue that is frequented by leopards. While wild animals rarely crossed over to human territory, there was always a good chance of Coco being caught off guard. He had never been on the hills before. There was a possibility that the curious dog would have got himself excited and gone to hug the leopards. Shrey had the option of siding with my father, but he made sure Coco had his entourage at the wedding. A person was dedicated to just being with Coco for all days of the wedding. And Coco was the flower boy at my wedding.

He made sure I lived my dream day just the way I had imagined it since I was a little girl. I never had so much fun and would, in a heartbeat, want to do it all over again. Just because I knew Shrey would be there with me, through it all. On the day we got married, I was so sure I didn't want to live an extra day of my life without him.

Wedding days are supposed to be perfect and the whole pressure of looking perfect can get overwhelming. I am here to tell you all—please don't overkill. I was working out for the wedding trousseau. I wanted to look hot. I was spending too much time at the gym, and I have had a back issue for the past six years. I overexerted and my back snapped. I was in a belt for weeks—through mehndi and other functions. The preparations were elaborate, and it wrung us dry by the time we reached Corbett.

Emotions can be so powerful. When I saw him, I felt resuscitated. On the day of our *haldi* and *sagan*,[42] I saw him looking so composed. It reminded me of the first time I met him—that day on the shoot. My heart was so full. We had an intimate wedding and we enjoyed every bit of it. We had no one who didn't know us. It was just us, celebrating our love with the people who care about what we share.

We danced to Govinda medleys. We were sitting amidst mountains, feeling the chill almost hit our bones. On our haldi, Shrey took a basket of flowers and poured it on my head. That's one moment I will take to my grave. I walked down the aisle with my father and that's how I wanted it. My dad handing me to Shrey made me cry. I was just so grateful that this happened to me. Shrey teared up too when he saw me. Men crying is just so adorable because so few of them know how to.

They say, marry your best friend. What they mean is to marry someone you can be friends with. Marry

---

[42] Pre-wedding functions.

someone who is calm to your storm. Who knows your triggers and knows how stop them from going off?

My most memorable visual from our wedding is when Shrey looked at me during the rituals and said, 'I am hungry, are you hungry?' I laughed, finally, after a whole day of looking like all the tigers of Corbett were coming to eat me.

I was unusually anxious that day. I was high-strung, sick, panicky, jumpy and mostly hungry. I had drunk a little on an empty stomach and that didn't help obviously. It took Shrey to understand the thoughts I was yet to coherently tell him. He simply knew it all. Seeing myself as a bride, looking at my life change more than I could anticipate, was stressing me out.

Shrey sensed that. Like the perfect man he is, he arranged for food backstage. We kept taking snack breaks and laughed a lot through it. 'Nothing enormous can be done without food in your belly,' he said. I laughed, he laughed, and we decided to love and cherish each other till the end of time.

I might not be SRK, but I absolutely disagree with the power of '*Ek tarfa pyaar*'. It's all nonsense and we should stop glorifying broken hearts and unrequited love.

There is absolutely nothing quite as fulfilling and beautiful as mutual love. I want to end this with a prayer for all you readers—may you find your Shrey too!

10

Notes from Broken Hearts

It's the last week of December and as I look at the year gone by; I see so much good that came my way. I healed, I found love, I got married and most importantly, I found hope that tomorrow is going to be better. Sometimes on our dark days, it becomes nearly impossible to find the silver lining. Depression and anxiety make it even worse. We don't know if it will ever get better.

I have rambled enough for the last many pages. I have laid bare my heart, showed you every bruise, and put across all the unfiltered thoughts in my dark mind, tricks of the heart and tips to power through. But then I wondered what made me write this book in the first place. It was simply to tell everyone to never give up on love, no matter how ugly, horrible and painful it has been. It was not love, but a person who didn't know how to.

And so, I decided to find other people whose stories of heartbreak will crush you and their strength to bounce back will inspire you. I wanted to name it *The Broken Hearts' Gallery* after the 2020 film which I liked, but then, I decided I am going to call it the *Kintsugi Wall,* inspired by the Japanese art of repairing broken pottery with gold. To remind you guys, that you are the gold that can make your life priceless.

Now, I must warn you—the stories are sappy and some of them are very sad. Get the tissues and let's roll?

Once upon a time, I was living what I thought was a fairy-tale with Rahul. We were an inter-religious couple, and despite the differences, love was our common language. We decided to take the plunge and live together, creating a life that blended both our worlds.

Little did I know that a storm was brewing in the background. One day, out of the blue, at the mall, I bumped into a friend of ours. He mentioned how sorry he was about our break-up and checked up on how I was feeling about Rahul's wedding, which was next week. I was shocked. That's how I discovered Rahul had been secretly searching for a bride for an entire year behind my back. Imagine my shock—he was getting married and I had no clue.

It felt like the ground beneath me crumbled. The person I thought was building a future with me and had been with me for five years was planning an entirely different life.

Heartbroken and blindsided, I had to face reality—one that left me grappling with the pain of a break-up I never saw coming. Love, it seemed, couldn't conquer the gap between us. And so, our once-upon-a-time ended, leaving me to navigate a new chapter that I never imagined would be part of my story. But I stayed alive, through a lot of depression. As I write this, it will be two years this week since my heartbreak, and I am planning to go on my first date since over the weekend. Fingers crossed!

May you heal.

Love, P.

J lost her parents to Covid and all she had was her boyfriend. But one day, she returned home to find her boyfriend in bed with her best friend. It ended, of course. But she wasn't working. She was on a sabbatical. She had no money and too much pride to let the schmuck help her out.

'I don't need anyone else's wallet to thrive, thank you very much!' So, what does she do? Girlboss alert! With the help of some generous friends and some killer ideas, she launched her boba tea cafe by taking a bank loan.

Entrepreneurship is no walk in the park. There are hurdles, setbacks and a whole lot of stress. But she was like a phoenix rising from the ashes of heartbreak. She discovered this crazy amount of capability she never knew she had. It's like she had a hidden superpower for dealing with business chaos.

Amid the barrage of invoices, customer complaints and who knows what else, J found her groove. She was resilient, bouncing back from setbacks like a champ. And here's the kicker—through the rollercoaster of entrepreneurship, she stumbled upon a rock-solid sense of self. No more defining herself through past relationships; it was all about J and her badass business now.

I was stuck in this relationship that was like a straightjacket. My partner was possessive to the point where I felt like I couldn't breathe without their approval. It was suffocating. I lost touch with friends because every move I made was questioned. I couldn't shop without his approval. If he hated my jeans, I had to return them. He wanted to decide what colour my hair would be, even the length of it. Texts were inspected, calls monitored—it felt like living in a fishbowl. Slowly but surely, my world shrunk to the size of his insecurities. I was isolated, and worst of all, I started believing that maybe this was what I deserved.

The possessiveness wasn't just about questioning where I was going or who I was talking to. It went deeper. Every laugh, every smile with someone else, was met with suspicion. It eroded my confidence bit by bit until I felt like a fraction of the person I used to be.

The relationship finally hit the rocks when he hit my father. But that's what it took to wake me up. It was like the sun emerged from the clouds after a prolonged storm. At first, I was scared. Used to being under someone's thumb, the freedom felt strange. But slowly, I started reaching out. Old friends, who I hadn't spoken to in what felt like forever, welcomed me back with open arms.

I started making new friends, too—people who didn't question my every move, who celebrated my victories instead of making them about themselves. The more I connected, the more I realized how much I'd missed out on. My circle expanded, and suddenly, I was a part of something vibrant, something real.

The break-up, as painful as it was, became my wake-up call. It was like permission to live my life on my terms. Rediscovering the joy of social connections wasn't just about having people to hang out with; it was about reclaiming my sense of self.

With every laugh, I felt a piece of my confidence returning. It was liberating. I found myself in these connections—not the version moulded by someone else's expectations, but the genuine, unfiltered me. Turns out, the break-up wasn't just an ending; it was a beginning, a chance to rediscover who I was beyond the constraints of a possessive relationship.

From a Fanny who is yet to find herself.

I was coming out of a failed marriage that left me feeling like I'd hit rock bottom. In India, weddings are a tick on the life list. My loneliness and depression were like heavy clouds that just wouldn't lift. I was asked what I did that made my husband leave me. Well, he left me because he found someone else. He fell in love, and I somehow got it. It felt like life had played a cruel joke.

I started visiting an animal shelter. I figured, why not spend some time helping. Maybe it would distract me from my mess. Little did I know those furry companions would become my lifeline.

There's something magical about caring for abandoned pets. It's like they know when you need a friend. The unconditional love they gave, their wagging tails and soft purrs, became my daily therapy. It was a solace I hadn't expected, a balm for the wounds that seemed too deep to heal.

One day, as I was cleaning out cat litter boxes (not the most glamorous job, I know), I bumped into someone—a fellow volunteer. After we got to talking, I realized we had more in common than just a love for animals. He had his tale of heartbreak and rebuilding. We became each other's sounding boards, supporting one another through the highs and lows.

Eventually, that chance encounter turned into something more. It was like life had handed me a script rewrite, and suddenly, I was in a more fulfilling story. Love found its way back into my life, not as a replacement for what was lost, but as a beautiful surprise amid a phase of rebuilding. The end of my marriage wasn't the end of my story; it was the beginning of a chapter where I discovered that sometimes the most unexpected detours lead to the most rewarding destinations.

Love,
Meera

So, my love life? It was with someone who was more of a tornado than a partner. Trust shattered; dreams trashed—you get the picture.

After the break-up, I felt like I needed a restart. I escaped the city. I couldn't bear to live there. That's when I stumbled onto this whole environmental activism thing at a village in Goa. Started small, you know, recycling more and all that. But soon, I was knee-deep in a mission to save the planet.

The pain from the break-up turned into fuel for a different kind of fire—one that drives positive change. Found myself planting trees, cleaning up parks, and practicing permaculture—basically, turning my frustration into something good.

This eco-friendly gig wasn't just about saving the planet; it became my purpose. Gave me a reason to roll out of bed in the morning, something bigger than my mess.

And here's the kicker—the more I threw myself into this green mission, the more I realized I wasn't just saving trees; I was kind of saving myself. Went from 'survivor of a toxic relationship' to an 'eco-warrior with a renewed sense of purpose'. I have planted 900 trees in three years. I am not averse to love but I am no longer chasing it. There is so much more to life than romance!

Noni

I was stuck in a relationship that drained me. My job was terrible, my home life was terrible. We had the inevitable break-up; it was long coming. I turned to cooking, not as a chore but as a passion. Cooking was my therapy, my way of saying, 'I'm the chef of my happiness now.'

But here's the twist—I didn't just stop at whipping up meals for one. I took this newfound love for cooking and turned it into a business. Yep, I started a cloud kitchen, cooking up a storm for people who wanted a taste of my culinary wizardry.

Now, here's where it gets even better. I didn't just magically become a kitchen maestro. Nope, I learned the art of cooking from my ex-girlfriend's mom. And guess what? We are still buddies and now business partners. The break-up didn't sour our friendship; and it all worked out for better!

Best,
Karthikaye

I'm Nitya, and music used to be my everything. I could pour my heart out through the piano keys. But then, life threw me a curveball—a car accident messed up my hand, and suddenly, my music stopped. It hit me hard. My piano just sat there, a silent reminder of what I'd lost. But in the middle of feeling lost, I stumbled upon something unexpected—electronic music. I wasn't sure about it at first, but I gave it a shot. Pressing buttons, and playing with beats—it was like learning a new language. Slowly, I found a way to turn my pain into something beautiful, something digital. The click of buttons became my therapy, and the electronic beats patched up the holes in my heart. With a little MIDI controller, I started making tunes that told my story, a story of picking up the pieces. It was like a rebirth. From the classical world to this digital one, I found comfort. My new music was a mix of old and new, proving that even when life breaks your chords, you can still make a brand-new song. I found not just a backup for my lost melodies but a whole new way to tell my tale. The tunes I make now say, 'Hey, I made it through.' It's proof that even after the music stops, you can find a different beat and keep going. Let's not curse AI all the time. It helped me.

My whole world crumbled when my partner suddenly passed away. The grief was suffocating. It felt like I'd never catch my breath again. I would look at the pillow next to mine and wonder if the pain in my heart would ever pass. I would hug his shirt and cry into it. But then, in the middle of the stormy days, I stumbled upon something that felt like a lifeline—his love letters to me. Turns out, he had written a bunch of them and never gave them to me. Probably saved them for our tenth anniversary. Each letter was a tiny time capsule, holding memories of our laughter, and our shared joy. My favourite one is where he talks about how he loves it when I fight with him because it gives him the chance to make up. It was like he was right there with me, even though he was gone. With each word, I could feel him beside me. Reading those letters became my refuge. It was like he was whispering in the wind, telling me it's okay to smile again. In those moments, I found a strange comfort, a reassurance that the love we shared didn't end with his last breath. The letters became a reminder that love doesn't bow down to death, and it certainly doesn't wash away in the rain. His words became my solace, and in those quiet moments, I discovered the enduring power of love—a force that not even death could steal away.

—Love, Rehmat

Harshi's *Pyaar* Guide

1. How to measure love? *Aasmaan mein taare jitna* (As much as there are stars in the sky)
2. A cuddle a day keeps bad moods away. Cuddly-puddly time is sacrosanct!
3. Pinky promise is the mother of all promises!
4. Never let the lack of a boyfriend stop you from shopping at Hallmark. Buy greeting cards, cute bears, keychains, mugs. Shrey is currently the owner of a few hundred teddy bears.
5. Be the daddy, not the donkey in a relationship!
6. If you don't spank your partner, do you even love him enough?
7. Love is always on the bed, never in the air. Have you ever seen floating clouds make love?
8. Fuck, Shuck *te* Butter Chicken—the perfect definition of romance.
9. Love hard, make love harder.
10. Prescribing make-up sex every time you want to break their head. Try it.

11. *Happy life ke liye kya chahiye?* (What's needed for a happy life?) Self-love, self-love and self-love.

12. Staying true to Orryhood—always love and be a lover, said the liver!

13. Use your dick, don't be a dick.

14. Jaise SRK-Kajol aren't a real couple, *waise hi* you and your male best friend aren't meant for that happily-ever-after. *Pyaar dosti nahi hai. Pyaar zimmedari hai*, which not everyone is ready to take. (Love isn't friendship; love is responsibility, which not everyone is ready to take on.)

15. *Kuch logon ke saath samay bitane se sab kharab ho jata hai* (spending time with certain people can ruin everything) and that's your red-flagged partner.

16. If he/she is bad at sex, then either train them or change them. Good for your mental health.

17. *Ek chutki sindoor ki keemat*,[43] Darling I am a nightmare, dressed like a daydream se pucho!

18. A successful woman is an appreciating asset always; appreciate her!

19. Once a cheater, always a cheater. You want to give it a second chance?

---

[43] The price of one pinch of vermilion: Reference to Deepika Padukone's dialogue in *Om Shanti Om* (2007).

20. Start working on the relationship if you expect the year-end appraisals in your love job.

21. There's nothing called a soulmate; the only thing you get to choose is a roommate—for life. Choose wisely!

22. Be your partner's permanent, loudest and strongest cheerleader. Because if not you, then who?

23. Three Ss in a relationship that will change your life:

    i. Sorry
    ii. Sex
    iii. Suno na . . .

24. Don't be a Joey; follow your moral science lecture—sharing is caring. You better share that slice of pizza.

25. If your dog woofs at you and woof-woofs at your partner, double tap the person because heart it is!

26. You can cast your love vote irrespective of caste, creed, colour, religion and age!

27. Cheese overload isn't just for your pizza; make sure it's also for your partner. Be cheesy and comfortable.

28. Marriage is not about love. It is about you choosing the same person every day, day after day.

29. Now that's the thing about commitment too. *Ek baar jo maine commitment kar di, tab main apne aap ki bhi nahi sunti* (Once I have committed, I don't even listen to myself).

30. Self-love is the best orgasm you can ever have! Try it.

Epilogue

1. Not every great date will be a relationship. Don't break your heart over it.
2. Until you are exclusive, you guys are allowed to see other people. It's not cheating.
3. Stop chasing the one. You are the one and you can be compatible with a lot of people. It matters whom you want to make the effort for.
4. Sometimes, it can all be wonderful. Two perfect people who are great for each other, it could work out on paper. But it is just not your time. Don't hold grudges.
5. Something not working out is not about you. Don't let your mind play games and blame you.
6. If it's forced, it's not worth it.
7. Not every right swipe will end up in the *mandap*[44] and that's okay.

---

[44] Wedding aisle.

8. Love can happen again and again. Love is a feeling, not a person. But relationships are a choice. Know where your heart lies.

9. In a world full of hookups, situationships, one-night stands and friends with benefits, just find that one person you want to go back home to. Every day.

10. In the end, it's about finding your reel partner for real. Ask your heart—whom do you want to send that home decor reel to?

You didn't think I'd leave without talking to you, did you?

Dear You,

I know you are almost disillusioned and on the brink of letting go. That explains why you picked up this book. You are holding on to every shred of hope you can, aren't you? I understand if this letter finds you weary from the trials and tribulations of life. When I started writing this book, I wanted to share a little piece of my own story with you, in the hope that it may offer some solace and encouragement during what can often feel like an endless and exhausting journey.

It's been a year since I walked down the aisle and said 'I do' to the love of my life. As I reflected on the whirlwind of emotions and experiences that have led me to this point, I couldn't help but think back to the days when I, too, felt lost and disheartened by the seemingly endless search for a person whom I could call home. Now that you know the story, you know I gave up many times over. I almost lost the love of my life because dating in today's world erodes your kindness.

The dating world is a daunting place, filled with uncertainty, disappointment and heartache. It's easy to feel like you're wandering in the dark, wondering if you'll ever find that special someone who truly understands and cherishes you for who you are. But I want you to know that you are not alone in your journey. I, too, have weathered my fair share of storms on the path to finding love. There were moments when I felt like giving up when the sting of rejection felt too painful to bear. But through it all, I held on to hope—hope that one day, my heart would find its home in the hug of another.

And then, when I least expected it, love found me in the most unexpected of places. It was as if the universe had conspired to bring us together, two souls destined to walk this journey hand in hand. In hindsight, I can tell you that if all the bad hadn't happened to me, the good would've never come to me. Every day when I wake up and see Shrey's face on the pillow next to mine, all the heartache and uncertainty of the past melt away. I can't over plan still because anxiety doesn't allow me to think too much about my future. But I know the vacations we will take, the dinner set we will buy and where we will eat this weekend. In February, Shrey took me to Goa for my birthday and I think it was perhaps the best birthday of my life. As my reels will tell you, married life has a few quips too and I am still making sense of those. Going into this, we knew I was not a quintessential girl. I am mercurial and moody, causing mayhem, but love has softened me a bit. I am no longer causing storms. I have learnt to be peaceful in love. I guess as the years move along, I will find out more about who I am and what I am capable of. But I now have one certainty for sure; my husband is willing to make space for every version of me.

You must be wondering if I ever think of the bad people and bad things that tore me apart. Strangely enough, I don't. Aman still lives a lane away from my house, and sometimes we cross each other on the road. The same road where we have so many memories together. But his presence doesn't register with me. It's almost as if he died for me when I moved on. I don't wish him ill, I don't wish him well, I don't wish him anything.

Maybe that common saying is right—the opposite of love is not hate, it is indifference. So, dear one, I assure you the storm you are feeling inside you is momentary. It will pass and the people who've hurt you will lose their power to have an impact when you stop caring. The difficult part is to make it from today to that day.

So, to you, who may be feeling battered and bruised, I wrote this book to tell you: hold on. Hold on to the belief that love is out there, waiting for you to find it. Hold on to the hope that each disappointment brings you one step closer to the love story you were meant to live. You are too precious to short-sell yourself. Wait for what feels like your favourite hot chocolate on a cold winter's night. And most importantly, hold on to yourself—to the unique and beautiful soul that you are. For it is in embracing your worth that you will ultimately attract the love that you deserve.

Geeli puchi and prayers for you,
HG

References

Shetty, Jay. 2023. *8 Rules of Love: How to Find It, Keep It, and Let It Go*. New York: Simon and Schuster.

Russell, Catherine Gray. 2019. *The Unexpected Joy of Being Single*. New York: Aster.

Elliott, Susan J. 2009. *Getting Past Your Breakup: How to Turn a Devastating Loss into the Best Thing That Ever Happened to You*. New York: Da Capo Lifelong Books.

Jones, Daniel. 2019. *Modern Love: True Stories of Love, Loss, and Redemption*. New York: Broadway Books.

Banan, Aastha Atray. 2021. *The L Word: Love, Lust & Everything in Between*. Gurgaon: HarperCollins India.

Boodram, Shan. 2021. *Big Dating: How the Tinder Generation is Changing the Meaning of Sex, Love, and Consent*. New York: HarperCollins.

Scan QR code to access the
Penguin Random House India website